TAKE TIME TO PLAY CHECKERS

TAKE TIME TO PLAY CHECKERS

WISE WORDS FROM KIDS ON THEIR PARENTS, FRIENDS, WORRIES, HOPES, AND GROWING UP

MISTI SNOW

PRODUCED BY ALISON BROWN CERIER BOOK DEVELOPMENT, INC.

VIKING

TO REEVE

VIKING
Published by the Penguin Group
Viking Penguin, a division of Penguin Books USA Inc.,
375 Hudson Street, New York, New York 10014, U.S.A.
Penguin Books Ltd, 27 Wrights Lane,
London W8 5TZ, England
Penguin Books Australia Ltd, Ringwood,
Victoria, Australia
Penguin Books Canada Ltd, 10 Alcorn Avenue, Suite 300,
Toronto, Ontario, Canada M4V 3B2
Penguin Books (N.Z.) Ltd, 182–190 Wairau Road,
Auckland 10, New Zealand

Penguin Books Ltd, Registered Offices:
Harmondsworth, Middlesex, England

First published in 1992 by Viking Penguin,
a division of Penguin Books USA Inc.

1 3 5 7 9 10 8 6 4 2

Produced by Alison Brown Cerier Book Development, Inc.

Excerpts from "Mindworks" and "Journal Juniors" articles
(Copyright 1983 to 1991 The Star Tribune) were originally
published in *The Star Tribune* and are reprinted
with permission.

LIBRARY OF CONGRESS CATALOGING IN PUBLICATION DATA
Snow, Misti.
Take time to play checkers : wise words from kids on their parents,
friends, worries, hopes, and growing up/ Misti Snow.
p. cm.
ISBN 0-670-84061-0
I. Title.
PN6328.C5S56   1992
081'.083—dc20   92-54079

Printed in the United States of America
Set in Palatino and Futura
Designed by Jo Anne Metsch

ACKNOWLEDGMENTS

To JUDITH ERICKSON and the late Diane Hedin goes my heartfelt gratitude. Without their imagination, "Mindworks" would never have occurred, and thousands of children and many more thousands of adults would never have shared in the beauty of the project. My thanks to the *Star Tribune*, particularly to Joel Kramer and Linda Picone, for recognizing the value of "Mindworks" and keeping it alive. A special thanks to Marilyn Hoegemeyer who has always respected "Mindworks" and for many years, nurtured it and me. Although his artwork doesn't appear here, I want to thank L. K. Hanson who gives "Mindworks" as it appears in the *Star Tribune* its unique visual identity. His art is bizarre, his heart is good, and every month I'm delighted with his transformation of a child's words into an indelible, eye-catching experience. My thanks also to Diane Knich and Matt Davich for their clerical support.

I owe immeasurable thanks to Alison Brown Cerier who realized so quickly what "Mindworks" was about. Her understanding of my passion, sharing of my vision and patience as I struggled made this book happen.

To my parents, Jim and Donna Snow, I give thanks for giving me a much better childhood than that experienced by many of the kids whose work I read, and for instilling in me compassion and tenacity. To my son, Reeve Schumacher, I owe a debt I can't repay. He has made more sacrifices than he realizes so that his mother could write about other people's children. A boundless thanks, too, to Jim Dawson for more than I can begin to express.

And finally, a deeply felt thanks to all the children who have written to "Mindworks," especially those whose words appear in this book. By sharing their young hearts and minds so openly, eloquently, and poignantly, they have moved adults in ways no grown-ups ever could.

CONTENTS

INTRODUCTION

FOR THE PAST nine years I've been immersed in a sea of children's voices. As the editor of a unique newspaper project called "Mindworks," I've read more than three hundred thousand essays written by school-age children about topics as diverse as divorce, God, aliens, sex, popularity, and grandparents. Every day I enjoy a rare privilege—being informed by those who know best about what it means to be a child in these times. In the process I also learn a great deal about what it means to be human.

The project had its beginnings in two University of Minnesota researchers' shared vision. In 1983 Judith Erickson and Diane Hedin approached the *Star Tribune* newspaper in Minneapolis with an intriguing proposition. During their research on youth groups they'd come across a supplement called "Journal Juniors" that had appeared in the *Minneapolis Journal* from 1893 to about 1913. Every week a question was posed to fifth- through twelfth-graders throughout the region, thousands of whom responded with very formal essays. The most interesting or best written were published, accompanied by an introduction by the feature's editor summing up the views of the kids collectively. Erickson and Hedin proposed that the *Star Tribune* replicate the project for a year, with the same questions asked ninety years ago. The *Star Tribune* editors accepted the challenge and the modern version of "Journal Juniors" was born.

I became editor of the project and was responsible for choosing the topics, reading the essays, picking some for publication, and writing a summary of the collected essays. Shortly after the project was announced, I began drowning in essays as children poured their hearts onto paper. It was obvious we'd stumbled onto a treasure trove of compelling, entertaining, and thought-provoking material. I was enthralled by what I read.

The first year we averaged 750 to 1,000 essays per week and the kids attacked questions such as "Would you rather be a man or a woman?" and "Was Lincoln or Washington the greater man?" The response was so positive that at the end of the year, we decided to keep going. The second year was much the same except the volume of essays, and responses from teachers and readers, continually increased.

In 1985 we decided we no longer wanted to be tied to the questions of the past because, although they were interesting, they weren't always pertinent today. As we also were struggling with the volume of weekly essays, which had become overwhelming, we overhauled the project. We developed our own list of questions, expanded the age range to include first-graders through twelfth-graders, made the feature a monthly one and christened it "Mind-works." Some of the material in this book has been previously published in those features, some of it has never been published before.

Each month during the school year, the kids respond to a specific question. The average volume now sits at around eight thousand essays per month, every one of which is read. The writers represent a huge range of kids from rural, urban, and suburban areas as well as from small, medium, and large towns. Students from posh private schools participate as do those from inner-city schools, parochial schools, and alternative programs for pregnant teens and dropouts. Kids write from juvenile detention centers, residential chemical dependency programs, and hospitals where they're being treated for bulimia, depression, or attempted suicide. Sometimes kids write from a special school for the deaf or schools located on Indian reservations. An increasing number write from home schools where they're being educated solely by their parents. Most write as part of classroom assignments, others simply write on their own. Occasionally I receive unsolicited essays from surprisingly distant places such as New Zealand, Japan, or Bogota, Colombia. For a couple of special "Mindworks" we included the work of students from more than a dozen countries, among them India, Turkey, Poland, Chile, and the former Soviet Union.

Every month a collection of essays arrives that's staggering in its breadth and its depth of expression and ideas. One moment I might be reading an essay from a six-year-old describing her sweet relationship with her pet kitten, the next I'm immersed in a teenager's devastating account of incest. Narratives describing healthy families are interspersed with painful stories of divorce, alcoholism, abandonment, and abuse. The kids tell secrets, make incisive observations about life in America, vent their anger, and express their youthful whimsy and exuberance. Always there are pieces that make me laugh out loud and pieces that shatter my heart.

Over the years "Mindworks" has become a well-known and popular feature. Disc jockeys quote it on morning drive-time shows; ministers incorporate it into their sermons; college professors post it on their office doors. Book groups have been known to suspend their discussion of their latest book to talk instead about the "Mindworks" that was published that day. Policymakers have distributed specific "Mindworks" to state legislators; it's been the center of discussion at board meetings of social service agencies and quoted by organizations battling abuse. Academic researchers have perused the essays searching for information about today's children.

"Mindworks" elicits responses from an astounding array of readers. A university student told me once that everyone in his rock band always talks about "Mindworks" when it appears. People without children inform me of how much they enjoy reading the children's words. Retired people write letters of admiration and concern for the children. And parents, expectant parents, and adults who work with children tell me they devour every word. Teachers frequently say they've never known their students so well as when they write to "Mindworks." Also, some teachers have told me that students previously considered "losers" suddenly garnered great respect when their thoughts appeared in the feature. Over the years, "Mindworks" has generated discussions between kids and adults that probably would not have occurred otherwise.

There is virtually no group, it seems, that does not respond to the perceptions and opinions of children who are being honest and open about not only their lives, but the lives of adults around them.

I believe there are several reasons why "Mindworks" strikes a universal chord. For one thing, the kids' writing is real. So frequently in this society we view children in two ways—as entertainment (the kids-say-the-darnedest things approach) or problems (gangs, sexually active teenagers, and educational failures). In "Mindworks" the children reveal themselves as multidimensional human beings. Their writing isn't glitzy, there's no "spin" on it, it's not generic. It's real writing by the kid next door, the CEO's daughter, or the factory worker's son, the youngsters we see hanging out at the mall, serving us our burgers, or skipping down the sidewalk.

While writing this book, I've received several letters from former "Mindworks" writers now in college who say how much "Mindworks" meant to them, not only when their work was published, but whenever the feature appeared. Through reading other young people's thoughts, they realized they were normal and didn't feel so alone. "Mindworks" provides for young people and the adult reader alike a sense of community. It's a monthly attempt to embrace all young people and recognize how integral they are to our communities and our personal lives.

While "Mindworks" is about what it means to be a child in today's times, it is far more than that. It is about what it means to be human. Every day I read the children's writing I learn about fate, luck, humor, differences in character, the pains of living, and the joy of experiencing the world. There is virtually no human emotion that isn't expressed by the kids—greed, fury, passionate love, betrayal, disillusionment, hope.

For adults, "Mindworks" is a way to gain new and invaluable perspectives on themselves—both in childhood and today. Any adult interacting with youngsters and teens who doesn't believe his or her actions and words are being scrutinized, is sorely mistaken. Through "Mindworks," kids both indict adults for their lapses, and tell of their deep love and respect for them. One of my favorite quotes illustrating this awareness of adults comes from

Paul, 12. In answering a question concerning the hardest thing about growing up, he writes, "The worst part is you are caught up in everyone else's midlife crisis. It can be very hard sometimes not to feel responsible for their pain. By the time you have entered adolescence, your parents, aunts, and uncles are in the thick of all of their worst struggles."

Throughout the project kids have offered memorable images only children could conceive. There's the child who believes that in heaven Jesus dresses up as Santa Claus every Christmas, and the young girl who can't wait to be a secretary when she grows up because she'd love to put people on hold. The youngsters often are generous with advice based on their own life experiences ranging from the sobering—don't try to commit suicide like I did—to the merely practical. An eleven-year-old boy offers this: "I've done this before so don't do it. Don't make faces at a Great Dane. The right thing to do is to run like heck."

The kids are capable of succinctly capturing the truth about any aspect of life. On the issue of what makes a good friend, for instance, an eleven-year-old boy illustrates beautifully why his friend is appreciated. He writes, "He is trustworthy, too. One time I left my baseball cards at his house over three weeks and there were still 832 cards."

At the center of their writing is a sense that their days are spent discovering what life, and they themselves, are about. They remark on world events and events that are intensely personal; they reveal their struggles with both the mundane and the profound; they express themselves as vibrant individuals who love to laugh and possess sensitive feelings that can be easily hurt. Often I'm struck by the children's philosophical observations such as those expressed by Dean, age 13. He writes, "Really, if you think about life, you'll find out that it's simple. You have hard times, you have good times, and usually, you make it through them."

In the nine years that I've edited "Mindworks," I've seen many trends, several of which are disturbing. In the early years of the feature, kids were obsessed with the possibility of nuclear annihilation. No matter what the topic, somebody wrote about nuclear war. That concern has faded considerably only to be replaced with a new fear—that of ecological suicide. In recent years young people have become well aware of the environmental dangers we face and write about them constantly. No longer do they believe that war will destroy humankind; now they see the earth itself as dying.

Often the young people's concerns reflect the trends in adult society. For instance, in the eighties kids wrote endlessly of their desire for material goods. Even the littlest kids wrote about having mansions and Jacuzzis and Lamborghinis. Then about three years ago, it shifted. Suddenly they began writing about social issues such as homelessness, AIDS, and poverty. A new trend is appearing, however. Whereas initially the youngsters expressed the idealistic belief that all of the problems could be solved and that they would be among the problem solvers, now more and more are expressing despair. Children of all ages are describing problems as insurmountable and many have concluded that the world is a lousy place and that the future offers no hope.

Part of this despair is related to the most frightening trend I see—an increase in violent attitudes and accounts of being victimized by violence. I can remember in the early years of the project how stunned I was when I'd read a child's account of the murder of someone they knew. In the first five or six years I saw maybe a half dozen such stories, including the essay that haunts me more than any I've ever read. I can see the essay clearly in my mind, an eight-year-old's penciled scrawl across tablet paper. The boy wrote, "Once my mom and dad were together. Then they had fights and my mom went away and me and my dad and my brother cried and my dad cried, too. Then my mom got killed by these two men and they killed my mom. And my mom is dead now." Such writings used to be rare, but in the past year alone, I've read dozens, if not scores, of essays from children describing the violent death of someone they knew. They write about a godmother being shot by an angry boyfriend, a classmate being raped and strangled on her way to school, a father being killed during a robbery or a student teacher being abducted and slaughtered in the woods.

An ever-increasing number of children say they fear violence on an almost daily basis. An eight-year-old girl recently wrote that she goes to bed at night facing her bedroom door; that way, if someone breaks in to try to hurt her family, she'll be the first line of defense and can save everyone. More kids, even very young kids, are telling about the karate and self-defense classes they're taking. Some have parents who are encouraging them to take classes on how to shoot a gun, not for hunting, but for self-protection. All of this fear is taking a terrible toll on their innocence; it's as if childhood itself is under assault.

A continuing problem I see revealed in the essays is the abdication by many adults of their responsibilities to children. The kids frequently write about parents who set no guidelines or standards and who are absent either emotionally or physically. Too often it appears that the children are parenting themselves and each other.

What remains unchanged from year to year, however, is the energy, wisdom, and delight of the young. Children are capable of describing the most amazing feelings and perceptions. Many of them maintain an innate sense of their value as human beings and as children, among them Tasha, 10. She writes, "With all the problems and hassles of being a parent, why bother? Because finding the Big Dipper or discovering a nest of baby bunnies would feel empty alone, but it would be fun and exciting to share experiences like these with your kids."

The kids write with a rare honesty, revealing their big hearts, curious minds, and enormous capacities for living rich lives. All children deserve the very best that all of us can offer them.

My most fervent hope is that readers of this book will be struck by the magic of children, moved by their insights, and inspired to examine children, themselves, and this society in a new light. If through these children's words people pay more loving, careful attention to all the children in their lives—not just those with whom they share their homes—these children's efforts will be rewarded a thousandfold.

MY
FAMILY

MOTHERS

Moms, take time to play checkers. — George, 6

WHEN CHILDREN WRITE about their mothers they write with gentle chiding, passion, humor, admiration, irritation, and sometimes pain. Birth mothers, adoptive mothers, stepmothers, mothers who overprotect their children, and mothers who abuse them—all are scrutinized by their offspring. For the majority of kids, their mother is among their greatest blessings, for others, she's a source of sorrow. But the prevailing theme is a positive one. Most kids feel a profound love for their moms and most believe their mothers love them, too.

This love, however, doesn't mean children don't see plenty of room for improvement. They willingly offer descriptions of what they consider to be "good" moms and rattle off advice on how to have happier, healthier children.

A "good" mom, according to kids, is one who pays older siblings when they babysit, keeps the kids away from Dad when he's grumpy, apologizes when she's wrong, and doesn't vacuum in the morning while the children are still asleep. She never says, "Why can't you be more like . . ." and she always notices the five A's on the report card, not just the one C. A "good" mom also isn't addicted to soap operas or the phone and definitely doesn't smoke.

"I've never met a person who's not been mortified by their

mother at least once," writes Keri, 14. That's an opinion held by many youngsters who have suffered mothers playing country western music on the car radio in front of their friends, moms kissing them in public after the age of 10, and anxious mothers grilling their daughters' dates with questions like "What kind of grades do you get?" and "Have you ever been arrested?" Many kids wish mothers would realize that the way they behave in the privacy of their homes might not be acceptable when they're in public or with their children's friends.

Many youngsters plead for their mothers to listen more carefully to them and never to simply pretend to hear. They want mothers to discuss with them serious issues such as AIDS and sex and to listen to their opinions without getting angry. They're hurt and frustrated when mothers trivialize issues such as peer pressure, friendship squabbles, and romantic dilemmas.

Most children relish their mother's affection and many crave more, including 11- and 12-year-old boys who write about how they love hugs and kisses as long as they're given in private. "Mothers should give you lots and lots of love because otherwise you will turn out to be a bum," writes David, 11. "Mothers should tuck you in at night. It makes me feel great when I am tucked in."

Ask a child to think "Mom" and an overwhelming number think "food." They describe mothers' cooking as wonderful or lacking and critique particular recipes. They especially love home-cooked meals for Thanksgiving, Christmas, and other holidays. They also offer plenty of specific suggestions ranging from no health food (one boy says his mother only feeds him "nuts and twigs") to: Never put an apple in the same lunch bag as a soft sandwich.

Household rules and expectations preoccupy many kids, especially those who tire of their mothers' complaints about the state of their rooms. Dan, 11, writes, "Quit nagging kids about cleaning their room. I know that when people see my room I want them to be able to tell it's my room, not just a guest room that no one has been in for five years." Some young people want more leniency, such as later curfews and fewer chores, but others practically plead for more structure. It's not uncommon for elementary-age youngsters, who describe the late-night television they routinely watch, to tell "Mindworks" they wish they had a set bedtime on school nights, and that their mothers would enforce it.

For many, their foremost request is that mothers stop yelling so often and so loudly. They describe mothers whose short tempers, grouchiness, and impatience infect the whole house with tension. A few implore their mothers to be more assertive with husbands and bosses; others suggest that moms not argue with husbands so viciously and often. Kids frequently attribute their mothers' bad moods to overwork and overworry. They recommend that mothers slow down, demand more household help from husbands, and give rest and play a higher priority.

Unlike when kids write about fathers, very few describe abusive mothers. Those that do write with profound anger and pain. Some beg alcoholic mothers to get help, others describe the agony of living with mothers who constantly insult or criticize them. A few rage at mothers who hit too hard and too often. Rarely do children write about mothers who have abandoned them, but when they do they agonize about why their moms didn't love them enough to stay.

On the issue of mothers working outside the home, kids write with frustration, sadness, pride, and deep ambivalence. Most kids expect their fathers to work and adjust their lives accordingly, but many see their mothers' working as a direct threat to their happiness.

For many kids, especially the younger ones, having a mother with a job means loneliness and a nagging concern that perhaps her work means more to her than her child. Some describe mothers who leave before the children go to school and don't return until late at night, or who bring work home with them. Brian, 11, writes, "If you do bring work home, you shut the door on your child." One result of mothers working, kids say, is that they're frequently too tired to play or be attentive when they are home.

Working moms aren't available to give their kids rides when they need them, depend too much on fast and frozen food, and too frequently miss out on their children's events. A junior high school girl writes, "I'm very proud to have my mom working as a flight attendant, but once in a while I'm not so proud, like when most moms are at a PTA meeting or all parents come to Open House and only my dad is there. I always feel like they look down on me and I just want to shout, 'My mom is a stewardess!' "

Many express pride that their mothers work, saying their moms seem happier, younger, more confident, and content when they're working. Working mothers are credited with being more up to date on what's happening in the world, less naive and more respected than mothers who don't have jobs. For most kids, the best benefit of Mom working is the money. Some, especially those with single or divorced mothers, recognize that their mother's income is what keeps them clothed, sheltered, and fed. For others, Mom's income represents luxuries such as trips to Disney World, skating lessons, and private schools.

Having mothers at work sometimes makes kids more responsible at earlier ages. Kids with working moms say they're more likely to have to help with housework, cooking, and caring for the younger family members. Some like this responsibility and believe it makes them more capable people. Others feel the same way as Angie, 11, who writes, "I don't like my mom working because she loads me up with responsibilities I'm not ready to take." A few describe how frightened they are at home alone after school or at night—they worry about being vulnerable to criminals or about not knowing what to do in case of an emergency such as a tornado touching down or the dog getting hurt. Children tend to be more appreciative of mothers who work part-time or the same hours as the children are at school.

According to some kids, a child's day care or after-school arrangements affect a child's reaction to a mother's working. Some write sweet tributes to day care providers who treated them with love and affection; others tell horrific tales of providers who were "bad news"—those who watched television all day, favored their own children over the others, and either ignored their charges or were constantly screaming at them.

Whether mothers work or not, kids ask them to keep a precarious balance: Be protective enough to show you care, but don't be overprotective and paranoid. Be youthful and fun, but act your age. Discipline us enough to prepare us for the real world, but be lenient and kind when you can. Expect enough of us to make us the best we can be, but never pressure us beyond our abilities. Always be interested, but never nosy. Know instinctively when we need you and when you need to back off.

Whatever their shortcomings, almost all mothers do enjoy the love and approval of their children. Many, if not most kids, would agree with the sentiments Kim, 12, expresses: "Maybe I do complain about my mom sometimes, but, really, I would never trade her for all the clothes in the world."

■ ■ ■

In order to be a good mother you must have: a child, patience, self-control, a warm heart, a soft hand, a big checkbook, and lots of love (husband optional, but recommended). — Jon, 13

A good mom is a mom who *does not* make you eat health food. A pretty good mom is a mom that lets you watch TV when you want to. A bad mom is a mom who will not tolerate mud pies. — John, 9

I like it when moms hug you and kiss you because it feels good inside. — Angie, 10

A mother should always carry Band-Aids. — Garin, 10

If I were my mom for a while, I would understand why she thinks I need to be able to play the piano and why TV will rot my brain. — Tara, 13

■ ■ ■

"Turn off ze Neentendo or I keel you!" My mother is like a Nazi when it comes to things she doesn't like. — Tim, 11

My mother cleans our house every day. It is so clean every step you take, it squeaks. — Ricky, 10

Mother, do not make me fix my bed because I sleep in it every night anyway. — Mariya, 9

■ ■ ■

Mom, I leave my towel on the bathroom floor for a reason, so that it's there for the next morning. — Katie, 12

She has to know that, to her, my room is a junkyard, but to me it's a place to go and not worry about problems.

— Paul, 9

Mothers worry too much (especially my mom). They get all stressed out. My mom worries about everything. She should relax and watch more television. — Sonja, 11

I would tell my mom to stop worrying about my hair. Almost everybody is growing their hair out long. She says it looks like someone who takes drugs, which isn't true. I remind her of all the country singers she likes who have long hair. She says when I'm making $1 million a year singing, I can have long hair, too.

I guess I'll have to start practicing. — Adam, 11

Don't try so hard! I think that many mothers try to be the perfect, stereotype mother. They're always doing things that they think will make their children happy. Some mothers get so involved that their whole world revolves around their kids. I say, go out and have some fun. Go dancing, you can afford to hire a babysitter on occasion. Just because you have children doesn't mean that your whole life has to end. — Sarah, 13

Don't exercise so much; it doesn't matter how skinny or perfect your body is. Your kids still love you just the way you are. — Robin, 11

My advice to moms is to plan one special day for your child and do whatever the child wants for fun. Only take one child at a time and don't do any errands, do something fun and special. — Holly, 12

When I was little I loved going on walks with my mom. We would stop and watch the caterpillars wiggle on the ground. I would look for shiny stones and fill my pockets.

My favorite thing to do with my mom was helping her make cut-out cookies. I would get to put the frosting and glitter on them. — Kevin, 10

I wish my mom would not work around the house so much so we could spend more time together doing fun things.

— Rachel, 9

My mom loves me a lot but sometimes I think she pays too much attention to my dog. — Randi, 10

My advice for a stepmother would be to be kind and let the kid think of his real mom because he might miss her a lot.

— Boy, 11

Buy at least one of everything that your child sells.

— Libby, 11

I would tell mothers to let their kids talk on the phone longer because if they want their kids to grow up and get married and have kids, they should let them talk to girls on the phone.

— Adam, 11

■ ■ ■

Moms, start liking those ex-husbands of yours. It would make your kids happier. — Megan, 11

Moms should ask you what you would like for dinner before they make you something that you had for school lunch.
— Adam, 11

You should continue to put us to bed at 8:30 because otherwise we get tired and then we have a bad day. Then we don't have fun in our day. We get yelled at because we are crabby. — Kristi, 9

The advice I would give any mother would be to teach your daughter not only how to cook, sew, and take care of children, but also how to fix the car and do other chores around the house. Likewise, teach your sons how to cook, mend, and clean.

In the future, there will probably be more single people. Kids should be taught not only the things their gender is supposed to do, but also what the opposite gender does. That way your son won't have to come home and have Mom wash his clothes, and your daughter won't have to have Dad fix the leaky faucet.
— Cheri, 17

Don't try to protect your child from the real world. It will probably end up doing more harm than good. — Kelly, 12

My mom does not need any advice. She knows what she is doing. — Emily, 7

My mom did a very good job raising me. She always gave me advice when I needed it and answered all of my questions the best she could. But the best thing she ever did for me was when my very best friend and cousin died of cancer—she comforted me. She answered all the questions I had as well as she could. My mom is not only the best mom she can be, but a very good friend, too. — Amy, 14

Sometimes my mom gets sad because I am a teenager now and she thinks that her little boy is growing up too fast and too soon. My advice is that everybody grows up and I think the sooner the better. — Jesse, 13

What bugs me the most is when my mother still calls me childish names like "pumpkin" or "my baby boy." Face it, Mom! When I'm taller than you, I'm certainly not your little honey anymore. — Mark, 14

Privacy is more needed and wanted as I get older, so when I shut my door or want to be left alone my mom shouldn't take it personally. Shutting my door doesn't mean I want her out of my life, it just means I need time to myself. — Jill, 15

Mom, I wish you'd please notice me. I know I'm not home a whole lot, but there is a reason. Whenever I am home you treat me as if I'm not there. When I get off work at night, everyone has eaten dinner and nothing is saved for me. I rarely eat at home anymore because of this. Whenever I am home and try to talk to you, you have something more important to do, or you are just plain crabby.

I even feel that you are closer to your other daughter than you are to me, which really hurts me inside. It seems you always have time to talk with her or solve her problems and that I can solve my own. I know you think that since I am the oldest, I can take care of myself. Sometimes I need your help, too.

— Girl, 17

When I tell you about something that is important to me, don't shut me out. When I told you that I want to go to an out-of-state college, you didn't even listen to me. You didn't even look at the information that I had. Try to be more open next time.

Let me be alone sometimes. Don't always try to push me to

be with someone or do something. I need time alone. This year is scary and I need time to dream about the future and figure out what I want to do. — Jenny, 18

Sometimes, moms, you don't give your kids a lot of attention. Then they feel left out, like if they're in baseball and you don't come to a game and in that game they hit a single, double, triple, and a home run and they get home to tell you about it and you just say, "That's nice, honey," they don't feel good about what they did anymore. — Todd, 12

My mom is very supportive, and is always believing in me —whether it be in gymnastics practice, a demonstration, or a meet. Yet she makes me very nervous. Because she has done so much for me, I feel I have to do great so that I don't let her down. — Elizabeth, 15

Something I would like my mom to know is that I hate when she criticizes my friends. I wish that she could keep her opinions to herself, and remember how important my friends are to me. When she talks about them and tells me things she doesn't like, I feel like she's disappointed in me. — Girl, 14

My mom should stop putting so much pressure on me to do things just like she did when she was growing up. If I was like that, I would be going around saying, "Peace" to everybody.
— Girl, 12

When I'm at a shopping center and it's crowded, when my mom and I are in the women's department, my mom says, "Lisa, would you like a bra?" in front of two million people. I wish she wouldn't embarrass me in public. After that experience, I feel about two inches tall. — Lisa, 12

Mothers, be cool where your kids are concerned. Please don't go blab about the "F" junior got on his report card to all of your friends while he's with you because it hurts. He is ashamed as it is. — Carrie, 14

Listen to me tell you that I love you. I like to hear you tell me that you love me. — Clair, 6

Hot buttered noodles—remember, Mom, when noodles could ease my problems or make me feel just a little bit better? I'm almost 16 now, Mom, and slowly I've realized that hot buttered noodles don't take the broken hearts, disappointments, disagreements with the parents, and the general feeling of depression away. The remedies of the past—snacks, a new doll, going through the tickle machine—are all just a memory.

I want to compliment my mom and all those other moms out there who try to smooth over the many wrinkles of being a teen. All I can say is to continue listening and wait until the whole story is finished. Don't minimize a problem, even if it seems small to you. Talk as if your teens were your friends, not your kids. Give them advice, maybe by telling a similar personal experience, and always end it with a hug!

— Renee, 15

The advice I would give my mother was when I was raped, she didn't comfort me enough. She never explained why he did it or helped me figure out how I could have stopped it. I thought I was old enough to handle myself, but I never thought something like that would happen to me.

My mother should have gotten a counselor to help me sort out my feelings because they were all mixed up. Also, she was never home. I had very bad dreams and she was never there to comfort me. About the only time she was there was in court, but by that time, it was too late. — Girl, 17

She shouldn't get mad at me if I make mistakes, because all people make mistakes. She should get mad at me if I don't learn from my mistakes. — Nathan, 10

I don't like it when my mom gets mad at me in front of my friends. She should wait until my friends have gone to talk to me. — Erik, 13

Kids are more sensitive than you think. They might look tough on the outside, but when an adult yells, they crumble inside. — Evie, 11

■ ■ ■

Mom, there is something I want you to change. It is to *stop,* *stop,* **yelling. It makes me get cold prickles. Please give me a warm fuzzy instead. — Boy, 8**

Nothing really gets me upset or makes me feel bad except for when my mom says we don't love her. I don't think she really means that, but then again she probably does. When my mom tells me that it makes me want to cry. I wish she wouldn't say that because it hurts my feelings. Even though we aren't the best kids in the world, she shouldn't say that. — Boy, 12

My mom has a lot of stress and tension in her life trying to manage a job, meetings, and, of course, two children. Sometimes she'll say that she doesn't love us and that she would be such a better person without us in her life. — Girl, 14

If I could trade places with my parents I would ground my mom and stepdad for five years and then I would kick them out of my house. When they were gone I would move far, far away and never tell them. — Girl, 13

My mom has a very bad temper. It isn't all her fault, though, my grandfather used to be very mean to her, so some of it was rubbed off on her. I also think that she hits too much. Whenever she gets frustrated, the first thing her reflexes do is take a swing. She just recently stopped taking swings at me just because I'm bigger than her, and she knows that I'm under a lot of pressure, too, and would probably swing back. — Boy, 14

Moms shouldn't hit. My mom's a foster mom so she can't.
— Girl, 6

I see violence every day. My mother has a very bad temper and if she gets too mad, she will throw something very heavy. We (my father, brother, and I) try to stay quiet all the time.
— Girl, 9

I worry about my mom. I used to worry about my dad, but now I can't worry about him because he is dead. My mom is a recovered alcoholic and my dad was an alcoholic. I worry a lot about my mom dying because if she would die, I would be an orphan. I worry a lot, I worry about my spelling, I worry about getting lost sometimes, but most of all, I worry about losing my mom. — Girl, 9

I wish my mom would wear her seatbelt more often even if I'm not in the car, so she won't get hurt or killed.
— Misty, 10

My mom died when I was two. It's hard to get enough love from one person. If I had a mom I'd be nice to her and treat her nice. I wouldn't be a bad boy. — Boy, 10

■ ■ ■

My mom stayed at home. Now my mom goes to work. I feel sad. — John, 6

Unlike most mothers, my mom works two jobs and that is a lot of her time. I recommend that moms only work during the day, then they can spend time with their family. I hope to spend more time with my mom because I want to be like her, committed and creative. — Hannah, 11

When I was little, my mother did not work out of the house. She stayed home with me. But now that I'm older she works. I feel I can get off to school on my own, but it's still lonely because only my pets and I are there. But they're always too tired to play. Sometimes I talk to myself but only for company. The reason I do talk to myself is because it's so dark, quiet, lonely, and scary. — Tanya, 11

When I get home from school she won't be home from work until about 5:30. I miss her in the afternoon because I always kinda had this dream of coming home and having her give my brother and me a snack of freshly baked cookies. There would be the aroma of cookies baking. The reason I had this dream is because my next-door neighbor's mom does it all the time for her child. — Kari, 11

I don't like walking in the door and my mom's not home. The television is not much of a mom. I can't ask the television for a hug. — Girl, 11

Having to go to bed and not being able to kiss your mom good night is not very fun. — Annie, 8

My mom does not like to work, but when it is payday, then she likes it. — Girl, 7

My mom works at home. She cleans house, she exercises, and most of the time, she grounds us. — Corey, 10

When I'm alone in my house I get scared. Acting like such a baby is embarrassing, but I get nervous. Until I was fifteen I never had been left alone. I think having a mother who is a housewife has really affected my personality; I'm much more dependent.

My friends can't believe it when I tell them I don't know how to wash clothes. "I've been washing clothes since I was 10," Kathy tells me. Kathy's mother works day and night; Kathy has to wash clothes. Since my mom has always been home with me, I have never been forced to learn. What will happen when I go to college? Then I'll have to learn quickly. — Girl, 17

■ ■ ■

I'm kinda a lucky child because Mom works as a teacher's aide at my school. It's like bringing my teddy bear to school.
— Mandy, 11

My mother works at home, but she's not quite satisfied. I asked her if she had one job in the world, what would it be. She said, "A veterinarian." I interviewed a working mother. She said she likes to work outside of the house because she enjoys working with other people, but when I asked her if she had one job in the world, what would it be, she said, "Raising my kids."

It was interesting the mothers at home want to work outside of the house and the mothers who work outside of the house would rather be raising their kids. I guess they're just not satisfied.

I'm sure glad my mom's at home. She made a good choice.
— Andrea, 9

My mother teaches second grade and I feel proud because she feels she can trust me home alone and it feels good to be trusted. It also makes me feel older and brave. I love her!
— Paige, 9

It doesn't really matter how I feel about a working mother. It matters how my mom feels. She has to do what's right for her. It's her life and I can't run it for her. — Michelle, 13

I think moms should work all day and dads stay home because we can play and we can play baseball. — Charlie, 7

When I grow up and am a parent, I want to be like my mom.
— Erik, 13

FATHERS

My dad is too rough, not home enough, he yells too much, and his consequences are much too hard on me. That's the way most fathers are. Why? I don't know. — Boy, 11

WHEN CHILDREN WRITE about their relationships with their fathers, it's very different from when they write about their relationships with their mothers. The spectrum of reactions is wider ranging, far more complicated, and weighted toward the negative. Many children write with passion, hurt, confusion, and anger as they describe men who too frequently ignore, abuse, or abandon them. Even many of the more positive and loving stories often exude an uncertainty that is rare in stories about mothers.

Everything about fathers isn't negative, of course. Some children paint loving portraits of fathers who call them from the office to ask about their day, who never miss a recital or a game, who stay calm when their teenager is learning to drive. Heather, 13, writes, "When I was a little girl, my dad would get me up in the morning, make breakfast for me, and do my hair because my mom had to go to work before I was ever awake. That was really special. I will never forget that." Others describe dads who help clean the hamster cage or assist with homework. One writes lovingly of a father who brings her crackers and juice in bed when she's sick, another of an adoptive father who learned to cook Korean food to celebrate her heritage.

But the overwhelming sense is that fathers are the people many children don't know very well and often don't trust. They also are people whom children usually love deeply, sometimes desperately.

Frequently the children describe violent fathers, ranging from those who only hit their kids "when they deserve it" to convicted rapists. Because fathers are often more physically intimidating than mothers, kids tend to find even their yelling and threats deeply frightening. "I hate those stupid threats I get! 'Shape up or your mother will have to take you off the wall with a spatula.' Ugh," writes an 11-year-old boy. A girl, 14, writes, "Don't hit your kids, that's the advice I'd give to my father. . . . Most fathers who hit their kids don't realize how scary it is for their children to know that at any time this powerful, strong force could hurt them seriously. Being afraid is no fun, especially when you live with the person you are afraid of."

Many write that their fathers almost never talk to them in any meaningful way. Part of this is because many fathers are rarely home and when they are, their attention is directed at things other than their children. Large numbers of kids describe fathers who seem to place work, watching TV, playing Nintendo, hanging out with their buddies, and working out at health clubs ahead of spending time with their children. "My father is almost always away, either working or playing a sport," writes a girl, 15. "I understand that he needs time alone or away from home, especially with my parents' marital problems; however, I can't see this as an excuse for running away from my sister and me. We are growing up, and once we are grown, we can never go back. Perhaps my dad will realize too late that he missed us."

When fathers are home, they're often tired and sometimes their only conversation with their kids is to ask them to make popcorn or fetch something from the kitchen. Frequently, kids say, when they do talk to their dads, what they get is criticism rather than understanding. "My father tells me to come to him sometimes when I have a problem instead of to my mom. But every time I do talk to him, he tells me what's wrong with the way I think instead of helping me. He doesn't help me. He only confuses me more," writes a boy, 15. Conversation is also difficult because of what many kids describe as their fathers' primary flaw—they are poor listeners. Some think fathers won't listen because they're truly not interested in their children or because they're afraid of what they might hear. Others believe fathers simply don't realize how important listening is to their kids or that fathers would like to listen, but they don't know how.

A fairly common description of fathers is that they're mean, self-centered, and bossy to everyone in the household. They don't help much with the housework and too often engage in cruel teasing. They also tend to jump to incorrect conclusions and frequently have terrible tempers. One girl, 12, writes, "If you're upset, don't take it out on us. We are not as strong as you think we are. If you're yelling at us we might be acting tough on the outside, but inside, deep inside, we might be crying a river."

Favoritism seems to be more of a problem with fathers than mothers, according to the kids, particularly the favoritism many daughters feel their dads show to their sons. "A daughter wants to get close to her father, but it isn't always that way. A father will never admit it, but he wanted a son," writes a girl, 13. Many girls say their fathers are willing to spend more time with their sons going hunting, playing catch, or working on cars together. They're also more likely to pay attention to their sons' accomplishments than to those of their daughters.

Many children are abandoned by their fathers who leave because of alcoholism, new wives, better career opportunities, or the problems caused by a devastating divorce and difficult ex-wife. The abandonment causes intense pain for the children who are left wondering if their father loves them. A surprisingly large number tell anguished tales of fathers whom they see every few years or not at all, of dads who no longer answer their letters or even call on their birthdays. A boy, 11, writes, "I don't know my real dad. I would like for my mom to tell me some things about my dad because she may hate him, but I have a right to love him. If I ever find my dad I will spend all my time with him and never leave him. If you're reading this paper, Dad, I love you." He ends his writing with a P.S.: "Put mine in the paper because my dad might read it."

The advice kids offer fathers is to stick around, open up, listen more, and tell their children they are loved through both words and actions. They recommend that fathers participate more fully in the parenting responsibilities and not defer to mothers or stepmothers on everything concerning the children. They want fathers who don't embarrass them with crude jokes in front of their friends and don't scream obscenities at coaches. Fathers, they say, should praise more and criticize less and be far more affectionate and playful with their kids. They should laugh more easily and never resort to violence. Many also suggest that their fathers treat their wives with more respect.

For some kids, stepdads take the role of father and they love them more than their natural fathers. Their advice to stepdads is much the same as that to dads, but they also add that stepfathers should not treat their mother as if she belongs only to him. They should also give their stepchildren time to learn to accept and love them. They should never try to buy that love. Unfortunately for some, stepfathers cause more pain in their lives by ignoring, bullying, or abusing them.

The yearning for loving fathers is a running theme through most collections of "Mindworks" essays. When fathers do involve themselves, the rewards are considerable. For instance, when asked to identify the happiest time in their lives, thousands describe moments spent with their fathers. They express the joy they feel in their fathers' company and the happiness they experience when their fathers even momentarily acknowledge them as important individuals. Delightful essays are written about fathers who have good senses of humor, who get silly once in a while, who act as if they are an integral part of the family. One teen remembers with great fondness the time she and her father had an argument. He came home from work the next day proffering both an apology and a long-stemmed rose.

There are two striking differences between the writings about mothers and those about fathers. The first is that children appear to know their mothers. That is, they could probably tell a stranger what their mother's favorite color or movie is and what her characteristics are as a person. For many, their fathers remain mysteries, men whom they barely know. The second, and most striking difference, is this: Most children seem to accept without question that their mothers love them, but many children seem uncertain as to whether their fathers do. Despite that uncertainty and despite the type of father theirs might be, practically all children profess to love their fathers in a profound way.

The task fathers have in meeting the expectations and needs of their children can appear daunting, but in essence the basis of the kind of father-child relationships most kids crave is really very simple. Jason, age 9, expresses it this way: "Fathers, be kind and gentle and hold your children every once in a while."

■　■　■

I love my dad and wish he could live forever and ever. I think every kid in America thinks the same of their dad.

— Jean, 10

■ ■ ■

I wish my dads would get lost because they both beat on me and my mom, sister, and brother. I don't want anything to do with them. I don't ever want to see them ever again.

— Girl, 10

Your dad needs to be funny to cheer you up when you are sad. If he isn't funny, you'll be bored all the time. If your dad isn't helpful, you might do bad on a test. Your dad needs to be strong so he can help fix things. He needs to be nice or your family will have a bad reputation. And most of all, your dad needs to be loving because if he is, you will have a good life.

— Kevin, 9

One thing I like about my dad is he helps me with my homework. He doesn't take drugs or spend money too quickly. Another thing I like about him is his clothes all match.

— Erika, 9

My father is a wonderful man. He has his fatherly routine down pat. — Amanda, 13

My dad is in a wheelchair and I think I'm lucky because he does things that some fathers haven't ever tried. For instance, when my dad went to high school, his mom was picking him up from school and when she was bringing him down the sidewalk, she didn't see the curb and she dumped him in the snowbank. They sat there laughing for ten minutes until some guy came up and helped her put him back in his chair. How many fathers do you know that have been dumped out of a wheelchair into the snow? Well, if you do, I think you have a very special dad. — Melissa, 12

If I could trade places with my parents the best thing would be going to my dad's work and doing surgery because my dad is an orthopedic surgeon and I would like touching things I'd never even heard of. — Holly, 8

I would like to be my dad because he is unemployed and he can do whatever he wants. But the bad part is, he gets lonely.

— Matt, 10

First, grow up, you're no longer nineteen anymore so try to control your urges to start hopping around the kitchen to Roy Orbison or Buddy Holly or that fat dude. No offense or anything, but how do you think I feel when a friend and I come walking in to see you and Mom twisting?!

Second, quit embarrassing me in stores by moving your arms up and down and around like you know how to break-dance.

I mean, how would you feel walking down the canned foods aisle while your forty-three-year-old dad is break-dancing like a chicken?

I'm sorry if I hurt your feelings, Dad, but it had to be said.
— Tracee, 14

I was wondering why you wear those silly California Raisin boxing shorts. My advice to you would be that you shouldn't wear them because they make you look silly.

And, Dad, some other things. Don't sleep with the pillow between your legs. Don't watch those golf shows, they're boring. Don't always get your car washed at the same place.

But, Dad, of all the bad and silly things you do, I still love you. — Tony, 9

Don't ask the boys I bring over if they want to look at your bear-hunting pictures. — Kelli, 17

My advice to my father is to listen to my grandparents. My father said he was good when he was a kid. My grandparents said he tried to start the barn on fire. My father said he walked six and a half miles to school, even when it was thirty below. My grandparents said it was two miles and during the winter they sometimes gave him a ride. My father said he had to do chores until eleven and he didn't get any allowance. My grandparents said he did chores until supper, usually didn't have homework, and he got ten dollars a month allowance.

The best advice for me is to listen to my parents. Probably the best advice for him is to listen to his, too! — Richard, 15

■ ■ ■

All dads should know how to say the alphabet backwards.
— Chris, 9

My dad should smile more in pictures. I think every dad should. — Angie, 10

I think dads should cook more and give moms a rest for a while. Because both moms and dads work, I think they should switch off doing housework. Instead of dads sitting around doing nothing but watching football and baseball. Dad should let Mom sit home once. — Alicia, 10

My dad should learn to cook some food. If my mom's not home, my dad just has a big bowl of ice cream and some cookies. — Heather, 12

A father should also keep the gifts that his children give him even if he doesn't like the gift. — Colette, 12

My advice for fathers is try not to hide the caring, loving, "motherly" side too well. Sometimes, more than anything, that is really what we need to see. — Mark, 16

Some fathers have this macho image. If they are seen loving a child, they will be embarrassed. — Rachel, 16

My father never showed any emotion like crying or even saying that he was worried about me. Ever since I was little, my father was a "Power Figure" or "The Tough Guy." Now that I'm older, I don't even know my father. I never really know who he is or what he feels. — Boy, 15

■ ■ ■

When my grandpa died, for the first time my father put aside his pride and cried. I'll never forget that moment when my father and I cried together. — Boy, 12

It is important for kids to see that their father is a sensitive human being. This won't make a kid insecure because they don't have a steadfast father figure whose every reaction can always be anticipated. It takes a much more powerful strength for a man to show his feelings than to hide them. I believe that this vulnerability makes kids *more* secure. They realize that their own feelings and emotions are okay. Because of this they don't try to suppress their emotions or to be someone that they aren't. They can accept and be proud of who they are. — Rose, 16

Dads should be more understanding, especially to boys. Fathers tend to think boys should always be rough and tough, when some boys like to be sentimental. Fathers should know that everybody needs to show their feelings. — Boy, 13

A father should have two sides to him—one for work and one for home. A father should be able to change his mood, come home, and have fun with the kids. — Melanie, 10

A father should be caring and ready for you to come to him with your problems. He should always be open whenever you need him for help. A father should be ready to help you with homework or math problems. He should always spend some time with you every day. He should be able to keep a secret if you have one to tell him. He can let you stay up late when your mother is out of town. A father should be caring and understanding if you're sick. When you're well, a father should be there to pick you up and zoom you to your room and throw you on your bed. — Stephanie, 10

One thing I like that my dad does is once every month we just have a talk. I like it because then he'll know what's going on in my life and I'll know what's going on in his.

— Adam, 10

To talk to me more. When I came home and helped him with the truck, he and I did not say a thing the whole time except,

"Can you hand me that?" He hardly says two words to me unless I bring up something that went wrong or got wrecked.

— Boy, 15

■ ■ ■

Dads, give us more compliments and fewer putdowns.

— Chris, 12

It's a lot easier to talk to a father who's calm and relaxed than to one who is about to erupt like Mount St. Helens.

— Josh, 14

My dad is the best dad in the world. He encourages me to read a lot and lots of people say my dad's really nice. When I was about three, I started to do everything like my dad. When he took a nap, I took a nap. When he watched TV, I watched TV.

Every night before I go to bed he tucks me in and prays with me. My dad can also make the best spaghetti and chocolate chip cookies. He also makes mint chocolate chip cookies! When I get in a fight with my friend or something that I'm crying about, he'll come in my room or wherever I'm crying about something and ask me what's the matter. At the end, I feel a lot better.

Every day my dad teaches me new things. He tells me what he did after work that day and says if he had a good day or not. Then he says that he really loves me. — Angela, 9

One time I regret is when I went to a movie instead of going fishing with my dad. I didn't talk to anyone about it because I felt guilty. My dad looked sad. — Jessica, 8

Do not pretend to understand your daughter's generation; she probably doesn't understand it herself. You may think that teenagers like "hip" parents, but usually your daughter's sense of stability will be severely shaken if you rock her world and show up at a parent-teacher conference with a purple Mohawk. Remember, you're the father; being a friend comes second.

— Amy, 16

Dad, when you go outside to play a game with your children, always let them win. That lets them have more confidence in themselves. When they go to school, then they have self-confidence which will let them participate better in gym.

Now, Dad, if you think it's not fair, remember, Grandpa always let you win. And he still does. — Jessica, 11

It was an intense moment for both of us. The air was so thick that you could cut it with a knife. Here it was, the sky hook, and he misses it! I had won! I had just won the first annual one-on-one basketball classic in the neighbor's driveway. It was the first time I had beaten my father.

As he walked home, he did not say anything to me except that I cheated and he really won. He dwelled on this event for the rest of the day. Now I feel like maybe he really did win, even though I know I did, "fair and square."

I guess the best advice I could give my father right now and back on the court is, it's OK to get beat once in a while. — Nick, 15

Dads in general should stop ignoring their kids. I know some will say, "But I'm tired after a hard day's work." Talking doesn't take that much energy and a hug isn't very tiring either.

— Corrie, 15

Every day football is on I hate it. He should stop watching football. Every time I want him to play with me, he watches football. — Boy, 7

I would tell my dad to pay more attention to his kids, because when he gets home, we eat supper. Then he and his girlfriend go upstairs and leave us sitting at the table. — Boy, 10

This past summer I was in the Color Guard at my school. Dad, you have never been interested in any of my extracurricular activities. All the other girls' fathers always would come to the football games and you didn't even come to one. I'll have you know that you really disappointed me. — Girl, 17

I wish you would go to school with me. I wish I could go to work with you. I wish you would take me sledding. I wish I could go out of town with you. I wish you would take me wherever you go. — Melissa, 7

■ ■ ■

You should spend time with your stepson because he might not have gotten any attention from his real dad. — Boy, 11

My advice to all you dads out there is to remember all the stupid things you did. Put yourself in your kid's shoes and remember how much fun it was to put that firecracker in the watermelon at the family picnic. Just think back to those kinds of things. Did you know you were doing something dumb at the time? Probably not. So go a little easier on us next time we do something idiotic like trying to do pull-ups on the shower curtain bar or spraying the hose through the kitchen window.

— Amy, 13

I learned to never throw a snowball at my dad, especially when he's snow-blowing the driveway. — Nathan, 9

A father's favorite word must be, "No!" because they are always saying it. — Jodee, 14

Dad, stop kicking my puppy. — Girl, 7

I'd tell him not to be so strict. It's okay for moms to be strict but not dads. Because dads are supposed to give children rides to different places. That's what dads are for. — Melissa, 10

The advice I would give my father and other fathers is not to yell too much. It will help both of us. You won't have a sore throat and we won't get mad at you. — Polly, 11

My advice to dads would be: Try not to yell. When you discipline us, try not too spank us too hard because sometimes it can really hurt. Don't drink or use chemicals. If we have chores, give us something if we do them right.
Why? I think if all fathers would do these things, it would help us to be kinder when we grow up. — Jeff, 11

My dad should be kinder to the cat and everybody else so that the cat and everybody else would like him more.
— Boy, 9

Give your kids discipline. Not too little so they're spoiled, but not too much so they're scared of you. — Christina, 11

The only advice I'd give my father and other fathers would be to treat their children as human beings. We all make mistakes. I wish now that my father had treated me this way. Maybe then I wouldn't have moved out. — Girl, 15

■ ■ ■

Discipline may help to train a child, but only love will make him come running into your arms when you come home from work. — Rachel, 16

My dad should stop hitting me because if I grow up to be a parent, I'm going to end up being a really bad mom.

— Girl, 10

I would tell my father not to lie to my sister and me and not to hit me. I wonder how he would feel if we lied to him and hit him? — Girl, 12

Can't dads just say, "Go to your room!" Instead my dad just grabs me by the hairs in the back of my head and drags me to my room. — Boy, 11

The advice I would give to my friend's father would be never slap your kid's bottom with a belt, because your kid will get really mad and will never forget and they will get you back when they are older, and man, they will. — Boy, 10

Dear Dad, don't fight with Mom. It hurts my ears.

— Girl, 7

When my parents got a divorce, my dad fought over the microwave instead of us. He fought a little over us, to make sure he could see us, but not as much as he did over the microwave. — Girl, 16

Dad, I wish you would have stayed around long enough to see me grow up to be the person I want to be. When you divorced Mom and left town, I finally realized how little you care about me. I'm not saying you don't care at all, but when you do care, it's about something I couldn't care less about.

Another thing is, I wish you could love me as the person I am inside, not on how I dress or how I have longer hair than most guys. It's not the attitude or appearance that counts, it's how big and accepting your heart is.

So, when you're ready to let me into your heart and straighten up your attitude, I just might let you be a part of my life.
— Boy, 16

I would give my advice to my biological father in Florida. Even though he has been remarried three other times, and presently has a son with wife number four, he should remember that I was his firstborn. — Girl, 11

I would tell my dad that he should move closer because my parents are divorced and he lives in Texas. I would tell him to have us kids go visit him more often. I would tell him it would be nice to send us birthday presents or even a card. I would tell him to write back to us when we write to him. — Girl, 11

I have been in a few foster homes since I was young and I've found that most fathers have a lot to learn. — Boy, 16

My dad does drugs and he throws my dog down the stairs. My mom and I divorced him. I've learned a lot about being a parent because I'm going to be everything he isn't!!!!
— Boy, 11

Dad, get a job and get a life. If you think I'm such a great kid, why did you leave me, Mom, T., and T.?
So, if you're using this newspaper to cover you when you sleep in your car, think about just why you left us.
P.S. Mom's getting married. — Boy, 11

My father is a dumb idiot. He sexually abused me! He would put his finger up my butt! He would also put water bags up my butt! He also abused my sister. He did that to me in some woods behind my grandpa's house. Some of the things he did were hit, pull hair, and scare us. I want that changed but I don't know how to do it. I have a nice stepfather now. My mom is nicer because she quit smoking. And my sister is nicer to me now. — Girl, 11

My father is an alcoholic. He has had a very hard life. His father was one, too. One day he called me and asked me if I wanted to go to the State Fair. I could tell he was drunk because of the way his voice sounded. I said, "No," and he said, "Is it because of me?" I said, "Yes, it is because of you." I'm glad I said no because I could have been hurt. — Girl, 11

Dads shouldn't do drugs because mine does and I never know if it's him and his actions or if it's the drugs. He really scares me most of the time. — Boy, teen

When I was young, my father was an alcoholic. His actions during that time were violent. He abused my mother, my brother, and me. During a time when I guess kids were supposed to be playing in the park, I was learning to be afraid of my dad. — Girl, 15

Yes, I do worry sometimes. I worry about my dad coming and shooting my mom and maybe my brother and sister and me. I worry all the time about that. It's really scary. The reason I worry about it is because he did cock and point the gun at my mom before. I just be careful so it won't happen ever again.
— Girl, 11

I try to love you but you make it so hard. — Girl, 17

My dad always tells me how proud he is of me, but it should be the other way around because he tries really hard. He didn't have a really good home. His father used to drink a lot and then come home and hit him. My dad says he could always

tell when his dad was drinking. So to sum it up, I would like
to say thanks to my dad for being the best dad he can be.

— Boy, 14

I couldn't give my dad any advice now because he died when
I was seven. But I do have advice for other dads. Spend as
much time as you can with your kids now, because you don't
know how much time you have left to be with them.

— Liza, 11

Dear father,
I want to thank you for all the things that you have ever
done for me. And I want to tell you this in a letter because
words aloud are hard to express.

Thank you for your love and the punishments that you have
given me, because I know that everything you do is for my
own good. Thank you for bringing me up under Biblical standards. Thank you for a wonderful mother, a neat little sis, and
for the food, clothing, and shelter you provide me with. I want
you to know that no matter what happens I will always love
you.

But most of all, thank you for adopting me, making me your
"little girl," and giving me hope for the future. — Lacey, 11

Daddy's little girl, that's what many people used to call me.
When I was little I did everything with my dad like fishing,
playing baseball, and learning to ride a bike. Then, my little
brother began to grow up and be able to do the things that I
was doing. It seemed that I was almost forgotten. After all, I
was a girl and should be playing with dolls and not fishing.
But just because I was a girl and growing up didn't mean that
I didn't still want to do things with my dad. My advice to any
father is: "Don't forget your little girl. She may be growing
up but she still loves sharing time with you." — Becky, 15

My father has provided me with all the necessities (and more) all my life, come to my games and recitals, and has been at my side since I was a baby. So the only advice I could give this man is to be able to let go of me as I grow older.

Of course he wants the best for me, but he has to understand I need to make my own decisions and he must trust my judgment. Everything I hold true, he has taught me. All he needs now is faith in the direction he has guided me and to realize the impact he has had on my life.

Letting go is hard, but little by little he will see it is not even a choice he can make, it is something that will happen—his choosing or not. So my advice to my father is, make it easier for the both of us. Don't fight "time," enjoy it and let me grow up. — Jodi, 15

■ ■ ■

My father shouldn't give me a good-night kiss because we're getting too old. A hearty handshake will do. — Wade, 12

Enjoy us while you have us because soon, you're gonna miss us. — Amy, 15

Fathers should tell their children that they love them, even boys. You might think that boys would not want their dads saying that they loved them. Being a boy, it is embarrassing sometimes, but other times I need comfort. It happened to me once. I was with my friends and I was going to spend the night at my friend Mike's house. Just before I left, my dad said, "Good-bye, I love you." I felt embarrassed, but I realized that I'm the only thing my dad has since his divorce. — Boy, 12

Fathers are wonderful to have around because their most important job is to love you. — Kristin, 10

SIBLINGS

I wish I could turn my big brother into a dog. — Alicia, 7

THE SIBLING RELATIONSHIP must be among the most ambivalent relationships in the world, one that can vacillate from intense love to seemingly intense hatred, sometimes within the space of a moment.

On the down side, kids write of constant teasing, lots of rough-housing (both in fun and in anger), and of fierce competition for attention and affection. They tell tales of pinches and practical jokes, of furious verbal battles and endless bickering about who did what to whom. Siblings, they say, are those who hang your favorite teddy bear from a noose or tie you up like a mummy, wrap you in a blanket, then throw you outside and lock the door.

Life with siblings can mean dealing with stinky diapers, broken treasures, shared rooms, bruised egos, and bumped heads—and fighting over the prize in the cereal box. For some, life with siblings means getting stitches, having chipped teeth and broken bones, and having your stomach pumped after your older brother tells you aspirin is candy.

The worst aspect of having siblings centers on the proverbial sibling rivalry. Every sibling, it seems, believes at least occasionally that the parents love the other children more. Regardless of whether they are the oldest, the youngest, or somewhere in between, practically all say they're often unfairly charged and that their parents practice favoritism.

Another common difficulty is living in an older or more successful sibling's shadow. They write of how tiring it is to be compared to other family members, how aggravating and hurtful it can be when teachers or coaches call them by their sibling's name. Many believe they will only be loved if they can somehow become a clone of their better-loved brother or sister.

Having siblings has its benefits as well, most admit. Siblings can be a good source for a loan, a lift, or stylish clothes. Most important, brothers or sisters are there to listen to personal problems that can't be shared with friends or parents. As Kristin, 15, puts it, "My sister knows a side of me that my parents don't even know exists." Older siblings can be sources of advice on wardrobes, teachers, and friends; sometimes they even provide physical protection from bullies. Having sisters can help boys to understand girls, having brothers can mean girls can hold their own playing football or wrestling. "A brother toughens you up for life. That way when you're older, if a boy bugs or teases you, you'll be used to it," writes Angela, 10. In many cases, siblings play a critical role for one another when their parents divorce by sharing their pain and reassuring one another that regardless of what happens, they'll still have each other.

According to many older kids, a special advantage is the sense that younger siblings look up to them. Both boys and girls write of how wonderful it is to cuddle with or read to or play with much younger siblings. They like the easy hugs, the silliness, and the chance to be nurturing.

Life with siblings can mean deep pain when a brother or sister runs away from home, dies, or commits suicide. Shalom, 16, writes, "I have lost one sister who died and without the other sisters, I couldn't have survived." They suffer when brothers or sisters fight with parents and get kicked out of the house or when siblings have drug or drinking habits that destroy the family.

The ambivalence isn't limited to those with siblings. "Only" children also express ambivalence about their families' structure. They say they don't have to compete for attention or the use of the bathroom and they admit they frequently enjoy more material benefits and opportunities. But they also express a deep loneliness—a situation some ameliorate by creating imaginary friends or "adopting" neighborhood kids or school friends. Many only children say they grow weary of their parents' overprotectiveness even as they enjoy more special alone time with Mom and Dad. They perceive enormous pressure to be everything for their parents—successful, well-liked, perfect. "Although it's nice not to have siblings, the price you pay is high," writes Brian, 14. "I have no person my age around the house to talk to. This is a much more terrible . . . feeling than anyone could imagine."

Given the interesting configurations of families, many kids have a variety of angles on the sibling issue. Their families include "real," half-, step-, former-step- and soon-to-be-step-brothers and -sisters mixed in with adopted and foster siblings. Some have half-siblings they have never met—they live in another state with a divorced parent, for instance—and most of them yearn to meet those children. Some are only children at one household and one of many at the other, the oldest at Mom's house, the middle at Dad's. Many, however, deeply love their siblings, regardless of the degree of their blood relationship.

One piece of advice offered to parents trying to rear a household of siblings that is common in the young people's writing is to love the children equally and treat them the same. The young writers also suggest that parents listen to all sides of the story before assessing blame and meting out punishment. Oldest children ask that their parents allow them to grow up and yet not force them to be overly responsible; middle children ask that they not get lost in the shuffle; youngest that parents not keep them babies all their lives.

Even though some of the kids' writing consists of tirades against insensitive, awful, annoying, even violent, siblings, most of the writers grudgingly admit that they wouldn't give up these troublesome brothers and sisters for the world. Chad, 15, writes, "For the most part I'm glad I have a brother and a sister. I can't believe I said that."

■ ■ ■

My brother is sometimes great and other times I just wish he would drop off the face of the earth. — Jennifer, 16

When I was younger, my older brother was sort of a role model. He taught us things that parents and teachers could not, like how to hide things in our room without Mom or Dad finding them, and how to glue a vase together. — Jeff, 15

When my brother was a lot younger, he was afraid of the dark. One night I took a sheet and put it over my head and crawled into my brother's room. I jumped up in the air and yelled, "Boo!" He screamed as loud as he could. I'll never in my life forget that night. It's great to have a brother.

— Jessie, 12

I have a younger brother, Nick. I think he is a bean brain because sometimes when I play hockey he sits there and yells, "Go, go," for the wrong hockey team. — Benjie, 10

I have two reasons for liking my sister Kelly: Sometimes she is nice to me (like she gives me shells and rocks). If I ever get stolen, Kelly can help me because she knows karate. The worst part of having a sister is when she is mean to me. Sometimes she pulls off my Barbies' heads and she hits me. When I do mean things to her, she does worser things to me. I wouldn't want to be an only child because I couldn't get to sleep without Kelly. — Kristin, 6

I like having a sister because sometimes when my mom asks me to do something I tell her Mom told her to do it.

— Julie, 8

I have one sister who is four years older than me. I enjoy having her around, but when I was younger she would tell me all kinds of ridiculous things. Since I looked up to her so much of course I believed her.

I would make my way across the street with a serious face, for she had told me if I so much as cracked a smile all cars had the right to run over me. That trick didn't last long.

Some of the things she told me were true. She made my life much easier by telling me what to expect at school so on my first day of kindergarten I knew the ropes better than most kids.

So what if I made a fool of myself once or twice in public, or got only half of the last cookie in the jar?

I enjoy having a sister because she is always there when I need her the most. — Jayna, 10

I have one brother. He is nice most of the time. He likes to look good all the time. He is 16 years old and he can drive a car. He brings me places. I like to play with him. I like him because he makes me laugh a lot. The only thing I hate about him is that he wears earrings! I like having a brother!

— Sarah, 8

The best thing about having a sister is having someone to play with and to talk to when I'm sad. — Christian, 7

■ ■ ■

The best thing about having a big sister is she can help me with my homework and I can talk to her. Like when my cat was lost she said it was okay to cry. — Brenda, 12

My older sister did something *really* special for me. The first day of junior high I sat down next to strangers at lunchtime because my friends had a different lunch period than me. So there my sister sat, talking, laughing, and eating her lunch with her friends.

Well, she saw me and noticed how sad and confused I looked, and she invited me to sit at her table with all of her older friends. "Is that your sister, Maureen?" her friends asked. "Gee, you two have the same eyes!" they commented.

I know other sisters would not do something like that for their sister. I couldn't believe how lucky I was. She doesn't do that kind of thing every day, but she did the right thing when I needed her most. I love her. — Kathleen, 13

I remember when my parents told my sisters and me that they were getting a divorce. My older sister was there to explain to me what was going on. My little sister (believe it or not) did help some, too. She was there to cry with me when she had no idea what was happening. The fact that I was sad made her sad. If it weren't for them, I would have blamed myself for the divorce. — Lynn, 15

The best thing I ever did was tell my sister I really, really, truly love her even though I say I hate her sometimes.

— Girl, 10

The thing I really don't like about having an older brother and sister is that they're always too busy to be there for me. I almost feel like an only child. — Cheryl, 14

The worst thing about my sister is that sometimes she does not want to talk to me about anything; she shuts me out and that hurts. — Emily, 11

■ ■ ■

Don't you hate it when your brother or sister answers the phone and to call you yells something like, "Yo, nerdface, phone. It's a boy!" — Leighe, 12

When you want privacy brothers bother you. When you don't want privacy, they give it to you. — Natalie, 11

Being the oldest of four children, I know exactly what it's like to have little brothers poking their noses into every detail of your life, no matter how trivial. You'd think they were planning to write a book someday.

I have often experienced what it's like to have more than one shadow following you where you don't want to be followed. I also know the feeling of tiny ears listening to conversations that later are repeated at the supper table.

Lack of privacy just seems to be something that comes with brothers and sisters. The more siblings, the more open your life becomes.

Not that I have got anything to hide, you understand, but sometimes it would be nice to just be alone. — Shelly, 16

■ ■ ■

Younger sisters always seem to be following you around everywhere you go. It's kind of like having a piece of lint stuck to your clothes that you can't get off. — Nina, 12

The hardest part about growing up is having a little sister that pinches you on the behind in public. I think my parents should put her up for adoption. — Shanna, 10

My little brother is a perfect example of a child I wouldn't want. — Girl, 13

■ ■ ■

Sometimes being the only girl with three brothers is reason enough to want to be an only child. — Bonnie, 16

I regret most the time when I tried to curl my brother's hair with an electric drill. The drill tore out his hair and he screamed really loud. Then I slapped him and ran to my mom.

The first thing I told her was to shoot me with my dad's .44 Magnum. Then my brother came screaming with a big wad of hair in his hand. Then my mom asked what happened and I said, "I tried to curl Brett's hair with an electric drill and it tore out his hair."

My mom grounded me for two weeks. When my dad got home he grounded me for a week. I got grounded for three weeks. My life was a mess. — Jerrit, 12

I regret fighting with my brother because now I like him more. I got real, real, real tired of getting hurt by us fighting with each other. It is so fun when me and my brother get along. Because now I don't have as much bumps or bruises on my knee, forehead, foot, and hand. So now I am a lot healthier.
— Matt, 8

If you ask my sister what's the hardest thing about growing up, she would say brothers. — Frank, 9

Kristina, my baby sister,
Today I stand over your crib in awe
I see in you
a marvel created by our parents
an image of myself
a second chance
to be what I couldn't be
to do what I failed to do
I hope that you
will avoid the mistakes I've made
grow up to
love and respect yourself
build the life that brings you
the most happiness.

Yet, just yesterday
I stood in this same spot
filled with resentment

Do you realize
you have taken center stage,
taken all the attention
for yourself?
How could you be so selfish
Kristina?
Why were you ever born
Kristina?

Kristina, my baby sister,
Today I stand over your crib in awe.
— Shannon, 17

The hardest thing about life is having little brothers and sisters getting all of the attention instead of us because they're little, chubby, and stupid. Grandparents and everyone pay attention to little brothers and sisters when they do these cute and stupid things. I'm sure I at least did cute things, but not stupid things, but now I'm too grown-up. I'd still like the attention, though. — Matt, 9

I learned that if we pray a lot, and if moms are on bed rest, we can get baby sisters. — Angie, 7

I have a half-brother named David and I like him because he sleeps most of the time. I just like him. I don't know why. I just like him. Maybe it's the way he smiles at me. — Ben, 9

My brother sleeps with a teddy bear that I gave him when he was two. I said he could have it for two days. He's had it for four years. — Carey, 9

■ ■ ■

Having a younger sister is only rewarding up until the time they begin to talk. — Eric, 15

When I was told that I was going to have a sibling (I was three at the time), I stormed out of the room and slammed the door. Four years later, my younger sister and I were told another sibling was coming. We were thrilled. We went downstairs and made a banner that said, WELCOME BABY.

— Nathan, 12

The hardest thing about growing up is that my brother who is five has diabetes. It is hard for me to see him get shots every day and we check his blood every day. It's hard for me to see him not get any sugar, get his finger pricked, and get shots stuck in his legs. Every day at breakfast when my brother wakes up, I have to hold his hand because he gets scared and it hurts when he gets the needles in his legs. If there was anything I could do for him, I would get rid of his diabetes. — Chrissy, 9

If I had a chance to be an only child I wouldn't because I'd miss those days when my little brother walks up to me and says, "I love you," and then gives me a hug. — Laura, 13

I feel I have the best position in my family being the middle child because I am close to both of my sisters. I can ask my older sister about experiences she has been through and then my younger sister can in turn ask me. — Joy, 15

I often hear my parents' tone of voice when they introduce us children. They introduce us as the oldest, as though they are the most proud of her; the baby, as if she is still a fragile infant; and the middle, just someone in between. — Jill, 16

The hardest pain about growing up is the biggest one always gets the blame or the lectures. The little ones only get said to calm down or settle down in a soft, sweet voice. The biggest gets grounded for a month in a very stern voice. The littlest get told to behave themselves in a very romantic voice.

— Casey, 11

Whether my parents know it or not, I think they show favoritism towards my younger sister. Say she twists her ankle. They would be all over her making sure she is all right. But for me, they just say that I'll live and don't even bother to ask if I'm okay. — Chris, 15

■ ■ ■

I think being an only child would be like being the only pea in a peapod. Lonely. — Joy, 15

The best thing about being an only child is you get more things, more attention, and you don't have screaming brothers and sisters driving you nuts. You also get more time to yourself and don't have brothers and sisters bugging you all the time, like, "Mandy, do this. Mandy, do that." You get better clothes (not hand-me-downs) and your parents' full attention. I just plain think that if you don't have brothers and sisters you won't get gray hair as fast. But still, brothers and sisters would be nice to have.

The worst thing about being an only child is you get blamed for a lot of stuff because you're the only kid in the house. There's no one to fight with, to help you with stuff, or take you places. You can't share a deep down dark secret with your brothers and sisters. If you don't have someone to play with, you could play with your brothers and sisters. — Mandy, 12

I would hate to be the only child because there would be no one to play sports or go hiking. That's why I make friends with only children. — Dennis, 12

■ ■ ■

I live in a family of thirteen. It is safe to say that I have never been lonely in my life. — Teresa, 14

Just before I was born, two of my brothers and my sister were killed in a car accident. Even though I never knew them, I know I would have liked them. — Girl, 11

Last summer my mom and dad broke the news. My dad said, "Your mother and I were going to have a baby but it didn't go the right way. Now we have to start over." I was heartbroken. I never thought this would happen to me. I'll never forget that time. — Girl, 12

■ ■ ■

"I wish you were dead!" A line often said to my brother. I hate to admit it, but many times I felt I really meant it. It hurts me that I ever said this to my only brother because he is dead and deep down inside I really never meant it. I really know it now that he is gone. — Boy, 16

I lost my sister by doing well in life. I was the one who worked for good grades and sports. For every accomplishment I achieved, she pushed me further and further away. . . . I would give anything to have her as a friend. I would give up those stupid grades and certificates. All those are are marks on paper. But I have lost something much greater. I have lost my only sister. — Girl, teen

In the past two years, my brother's and my relationship started to fade away because of his drug problem. I thought I was being his best friend by covering up for him, lying for him, and borrowing him money. It took me these past two years to realize that the only way to really help him would be to quit covering up for him, lying for him, and borrowing him money. This was very hard for me to do. I had to take the risk of losing our special friendship. I hope my brother realizes that I was only trying to help him, not hurt him. — Girl, 15

■ ■ ■

Sometimes when I watch my mom or dad hug their brothers or sisters, I wonder if my brother and I will ever hug each other. — Amanda, 9

Every now and then, my fellow siblings slip up, intentionally or otherwise. At that moment, my sister says in plain old everyday English, "I love you." My baby brother voices a similar, yet not quite so English, "I lub lou," and in an outpouring of emotion, my two other brothers utter, "You're okay." Tender moments like these are almost enough to make me say something nice about my brothers and sisters. Almost enough, but not quite. — Megan, 18

GRANDPARENTS

Both of my grandmas taught me the importance of playing Bingo. — Kim, 13

NEVER IN NINE years has "Mindworks" been deluged by so many love letters as when the topic was grandparents. The vast majority of the essays are sweet and tender tributes to grandparents both living and dead.

The sentiments are surprising considering the grim responses several years ago to a question about what it would be like to become elderly: tales of suffering in nursing homes, being lonely and rejected and becoming, as one put it, like a child again—someone no one listens to. When children write about being old not as an abstraction but in terms of real people they know well, though, their tone changes to respect, love, even awe.

Grandparents, say most kids, treat children as if they are truly special. They find time when parents can't—or don't—to cuddle, weave magical tales, ask questions, and, above all, listen. They spoil grandchildren by indulging them with gifts and breaking the household rules. They shower grandkids with praise and continually remind them in words and actions that they are loved.

Mention grandmas, and, as with mothers, many kids think *food:* the scent of fresh cinnamon rolls wafting from the kitchen, platters and bowls overflowing with roast beef and potatoes and gravy, that holiday bread or special enchilada, those reliable candy dishes and cookie jars. One grandma earned the appellation "Grandma Turkey" because of her succulent offering every Thanksgiving.

Youngsters revel in curling up on grandparents' laps and learning about who their parents really are—imperfect adults who once were children too. They delight in hearing the tales of their parents' childhood struggles and shenanigans. Grandparents also give invaluable insight into their heritage and history, say many, as they help grandchildren make jingle dresses for powwows or teach them languages like Yiddish, Latvian, or Chinese. Hundreds relate how much they love their grandpas' war stories and anecdotes about the Great Depression. One admits that when she was young she always thumped on her grandpa's wooden leg, the result of a war injury, to add emphasis to her knock-knock jokes. Another has learned from her grandfather never to complain about food—he survived a concentration camp only because a little girl sneaked him raw chicken livers.

Thousands describe simple joys they've learned from grandparents, from playing cards to fishing to quilting. Through grandparents many also learn their most difficult lessons about life and death. They discover how much it hurts to lose someone they love, how heartbreaking it is to watch a loved one deteriorate from Alzheimer's disease. They also learn about strength and dignity when they observe grandparents who show grace in the midst of pain and adversity.

For some, grandparents provide a rare and hopeful message about the possibility of lifelong marriages; others learn that grandparents, too, divorce. They must adapt to stepgrandparents, some of whom quickly become loved, others quickly despised. It is especially unforgivable, a couple of children say, when a stepgrandparent forbids a grandparent to maintain a special relationship with his or her grandchildren.

Among the most surprising revelations in the collection is the depth of love many teenage boys feel for their grandparents. With no other topic have they written with such unabashed emotion. Greg, 15, writes: "My grandma smells so beautiful. She smells just like a dozen fresh roses." Others tell of taking Grandma's arm as she walks because she suffers so from arthritis, of speaking up to make sure she can hear them. They write with deep pride of grandfathers who are their heroes.

"One thing I regret is not ever telling my grandpa I love him. Now that I'm fifteen I think it's too late, but it's not. I just can't tell him, even though I do love him," writes Andy.

Although most kids describe warm relationships with grandparents who enhance their lives, not all are so lucky. Dozens write of alcoholic grandparents who are "mean and stupid" when they get drunk. Several express the pain they experience because of lingering family feuds that prevent closeness with grandparents. Deep heartache is expressed by those who have grandparents who ignore them, who favor siblings or cousins over them, who substitute presents and money for the most desired gift of all, time. "When I think of my grandmother I think of a sweet, sincere person who just hasn't taken the time to go to her grandchildren's church or school programs," writes one teenager. "I don't think she does it intentionally; she just doesn't know how much we really want her there."

The majority have known at least one grandparent, but some have enjoyed as many as eight, given divorces, deaths, and remarriages. For many, Grandma is as close as next door or across town while others yearn for grandparents living halfway around the world. Scores describe lives spent living with grandparents because of the death, divorce, drug abuse, or neglect of their parents. For many kids, the stability and comfort grandparents provided enabled them to survive the devastation of their parents' divorce.

Children overflow with love and memories of grandparents who have shared their lives. As April, 10, says, it is "a special relationship I have with no one else in this world."

■ ■ ■

When I was little my grandpa and I were best friends. When I was about five we would go to the lake cabin. My grandpa and I would take the big boat all over the lake and scare my family that was fishing.

The next year or so my grandpa had a stroke and had to have his lung removed. We thought he was going to die so I brought my grandpa a lucky bunny. I thought it would make him not die. The next year we sold the cabin, but we would see grandpa at his house.

This year my grandpa passed away. The day he died I left school early to try to make it to Iowa to see him before he died. We made it. When I saw him I told him a joke and gave him his last laugh.

At his funeral I put the lucky bunny in his casket; now he is buried with his bunny. — Brian, 13

Some weekends, I used to stay there just because it was so fun. We used to always make cookies, oatmeal ones. While we made them, my grandpa used to hold my dolls for me because I thought they would cry if he didn't. — Danielle, 15

Whenever I did not drink my milk my grandpa would drink it for me. Grandparents are wonderful. — Betsy, 11

■ ■ ■

My grandmother is a woman who loves nature. She loves to catch frogs, pick flowers, and stand on her head.
— Elisabeth, 10

My grandma does a lot of things for me. She always took a walk with me when I wanted to take one. I give her hugs and kisses. It's like a trade, she does something for me and I do something for her. She does not do any sports. She just jogs around the block. She is very fun. I bet you would like to meet her. — James, 8

■ ■ ■

My grandpa took me out to the barn to find some kittens and he took me without even finishing his coffee. Most adults usually finish their coffee before they do anything.

— Carrie, 10

My grandpa is like a comedian waiting to go onstage. If my grandma stops talking long enough to let him get a word in, he is one of the funniest people I know. If he didn't have such a great sense of humor, I'm sure he would have divorced my grandma after the first week. — Ann, 15

Grandparents are the people that make your heart feel at home no matter what you do. — Jenny, 15

I can trust my grandpa with every secret I have and no matter how bad, private, or drastic it is, I know he won't breathe a word of it. That's one reason why I love my grandpa, because I can tell him things I can't tell anybody else, not even my mom. — Angel, 12

My grandparents always listen to my conversations and let me know by their hugs that I am special. I am very proud to be half Chinese and follow some of the Chinese customs my grandparents have taught me.

When it is time to say good-bye to Popo and Kan Kan and come back to Minnesota, my heart always cries a lot even though my eyes don't show the tears. — Bret, 11

I tried waterskiing and got up for a few seconds. When I fell, my grandparents clapped the loudest and I felt proud!

— Molly, 8

■ ■ ■

My grandma keeps me healthy by cooking roast beef, mashed potatoes, and gravy (my favorite). My grandpa entertains me by yodeling. — Amy, 11

Whenever Mom says, "No," I can count on Nana to say, "Yes." When I wanted to get a stuffed animal, Mom said, "No, she has enough." Nana said, "I'll get it for you."

Mommy's job is to teach me that I can't have everything I want. I know that now. Nana's job is to love me even when I'm wrong.

I'm glad that I have both a mommy and Nana. — Andrea, 9

Grandparents are great. They're the ones who cart you around when you can't find a ride. They're the ones who persuade your parents to let you stay out later or persuade your parents to unground you. They tell the truth and talk to you like you're an adult and not some stupid little kid that doesn't understand a thing you're saying. They're the extra parent you need when yours are at work or mad at you. — Cory, 14

My grandma always asks me how I'm doing and she means it. She talks to me always in a very happy voice. That makes me feel loved. Wouldn't you?

My best time with my grandma was this summer when I was alone with her at her house in Wisconsin. She let me come without my sisters. That made me feel special. When I was there I felt happy and proud and safe. — Evan, 7

Say you put three cups of salt in Grandma's homemade cookies and find out afterwards that the recipe called for sugar, or you spilled Kool-Aid all over Grandpa's suit, your head was still on your shoulders. Grandma didn't throw the cookies out in front of you to make you feel bad. She waited until you left the room and Grandpa would say to you, "That's all right, son, it was just an accident." — Travis, 14

My grandma is the one that everyone runs to hug as soon as they get in the door. But, everyone loves my grandpa just as much. I sometimes worry that maybe he doesn't know that. — Becki, 14

During seasons other than summer, my grandparents amaze me with the various lifestyles they live. For instance, when I was in kindergarten, my grandparents lived in Africa for two years. When they returned, not only did they bring back many souvenirs, they also brought back an African boy who was about four years older than me. They brought him back because he had polio in his left leg and it required surgery. When all the surgery was completed, he was a new boy. He had come to the United States speaking only African. He was used to sleeping on the dirt ground and wearing no clothes. That had been his culture and he now was used to ours. It would be hard for him to go back so my grandparents adopted him. I now know him as my Uncle Etim.

It means a lot to me to know I have such thoughtful and caring grandparents, and I will always admire their generosity and desire to help others. — Jennifer, 14

When I see my grandparents, it's a lot of fun because they are all party animals. My grandpa, even with two fake knees, can still dance all night. — Nick, 13

My grandparents (on my mom's side) and I get along great, even though I'm at these difficult teenage years when family is "nerdy." I think the main reason we get along so well is that I respect them and they also respect me. — Ali, 14

It was always a long drive down the twisted country roads, and although we usually arrived late, they were always waiting. My grandparents, like many others, lived on a farm in southern Minnesota. It was a wonderful farm. I always enjoyed exploring the many buildings over and over.

There was a wonderful garden between the hog house and the barn. I remember my Saturday morning outings with my grandma. In the early morning hours, we'd go to pick ripe strawberries. We'd always start out with a lot, but by the time we returned to the house, there would be hardly any left in the basket.

We always ate heartily. Grandma is a great cook, and she's always ready to stuff us, no matter what time it is. Then, at night, we'd go outside with our ice cream and look at the bright stars shining in the clear black night. Everything was so fresh and pure.

Then something happened. It was as if the slightest thing would set me off like a rocket. I became really irritable and cranky when it was time to visit Grandma and Grandpa (most people call it puberty). Whenever we were there, I was bored and pouted when I didn't get my way. I ignored my grandparents and was rude. It's not that I meant to be, but it seemed as if I just couldn't stop myself.

This went on for a few years, and then I finally noticed a change. I was maturing and suddenly, the idea of going to the boonies to visit Grandma and Grandpa wasn't so unappealing anymore. It gave me time to be alone and catch up on my sleep.

Now it really doesn't bother me. I like visiting with them, listening to their stories again. I know they have noticed my major attitude change, and are surprised. I only wished I hadn't wasted all that time being an obstinate brat. — Sarah, 15

My mom and dad are dead. My dad died before I was born. My mom died when I was three. I have lived with my grandma ever since, and it has been fun.

We go to a lot of movies. We go to my brother's house. My brother and I go to the park and play catch with a football. When I played football, Grandma was always cheering the team on, even in the rain and cold. This fall, I hope she does the same.

Every summer we go on a vacation. It's usually to Iowa. This summer we went to Texas. That was my first time to fly. I'm glad I have a grandma. — Andy, 10

Most people think of school as a boring place. I used to, too, but, because of my grandma, I have turned my opinion around completely.

I remember sitting in my grandma's living room listening to her read poetry. "This one always made your Aunt Mary cry," she would say. This would catch my attention. I would wonder how a poem could make my aunt cry. I listened carefully and discovered how beautiful the poem really was. I'd want to read more and more.

I remember her handing me these old, brown books that smelled of musty basements and I would flinch, thinking they would contain words like "thee" and "thou." Now those wonderful old books line my shelves.

Grandma showed me yearbooks, newspaper clippings, and miscellaneous objects she had collected in "her day." These always got me doing research, only to discover how incredibly interesting "her day" was.

Grandma thought of such clever ways to get me studying. She'd challenge me to games of Boggle only to let me win so I would think I was some spelling and vocabulary whiz. I would go back to school and work extra-hard on these subjects so Grandma could be even prouder of me.

In all these ways, my grandma showed me how much fun learning is. Well, Grandma, it worked. You've got one granddaughter who loves learning and appreciates you so much for helping her discover all the good things education holds.

— Stephanie, 16

I love it when my grandmother tells stories to me about her life because it sounds like a carefree time. And in this world with all the hate, the wars, the crime, the death, and the sadness that goes on every day, these stories need to be heard.

— Patt, 11

My grandparents aren't that "grand" at all. The only thing they taught me is that grandparents don't always love everyone. I can remember numerous times that my grandparents told my cousins that they loved them. They never once said that to me or my sister. But I don't really mind. I don't think I love them either. — Girl, 12

I have mixed feelings about how my grandparents have affected my life. When I was four and a half, I was adopted. My dad worked full time and my mom went to school so I stayed with my grandparents during the day.

It took me until I was nine to figure out that my grandpa was sexually molesting me. It took me until age sixteen to tell someone—my school counselor, then my parents. The worst part is I still must see my grandparents once a week. My grandmother has no idea about what went on. She is a wonderful person and I know she cares about me.

What I've gained from my grandparents' involvement is a love/hate relationship. Although I forgive my grandpa for what he has done, I have a feeling of hatred for him deep down inside. — Girl, 16

My grandpa has played an important role in my life because I lost my dad when I was one year old. He has been like a father to me.

Now my grandpa is in a wheelchair and cannot talk. But, I think if he could do what he used to do, he would still help me out a lot. Now I help him out and it makes me feel real good because he helped me when I needed help. — Mark, 12

My grandpa can't do much with me because he is in a nursing home, but I just enjoy the way he talks to me. He likes to hold my hand a lot and sometimes he even tells me that he loves me. That makes me feel great. I love my grandpa and I'm sure he loves me. — Traci, 8

You can really learn a lot from them and you can learn a lot about your parents. Like, how my dad ran over a shed with a bulldozer, and how my mom dressed her dog like Cleopatra.
— Brendan, 11

My father's mother was a farm wife. From her I learned never to tire of hard work. Anyone who could draw my grandmother a horse was a real artist. I was taught to clean my plate or the sun wouldn't shine the next day. Dad's father encouraged me to read the *National Geographic* magazine because in his opinion it's the best magazine in print. He told me never to buy anything in an airport—it costs more than at home. Rice Krispies are the ideal breakfast food. I learned never to overstay my welcome.

My mother's parents enjoy traveling and their TV is usually turned to CNN. Grandma is a fantastic seamstress who is never idle and has taught me there is no excuse for boredom.

A few of the things I've learned from my gramps are: Be patient. Be polite. Golf is a lot like life. Read the newspaper. Support your community. Volunteer. Take a walk every day. Be more concerned with others than yourself. Play card games—they improve your mind. If you're tired, take a nap. If it's cold, wear a scarf and cap. Peanuts and beer are staple foods. Be calm. Be friendly. Be proud of your accomplishments.
— Greta, 16

■ ■ ■

"You only live once," my grandma told me when I was in sixth grade and really nervous at a dance competition. She told me to, "Shake what your grandma gave you." — Jennifer, 14

I learned, from her experience, that it is hard for women in the business world, although she has told me that with education and a college degree, I can get somewhere in the world today. From notebooks to clothes, my grandmother makes sure I have everything for school.

There's a saying she always told me to remember: 30/30, which means $30,000 a year and for me to wait until at least age 30 to think about marriage and kids. — Malaika, 14

From them, I learned that I have a lot to learn because the real world isn't all smiles. In the real world, my grandparents work very hard and get a lot of owies. — Jaclyn, 9

My mom's dad is nothing like my other grandparents because he taught me a lesson never to smoke. If I do smoke, as he did, I will never grow to see my grandchildren because he didn't. — Larke, 9

My grandma and grandpa are very special to me and have played a big role in my life. I have cerebral palsy and have to use a wheelchair to get around and a special computer and a word board to help me talk. My grandma gives me massages sometimes. The massage feels good and helps me relax.

While Grandma gives me the massage, Grandpa tells me stories about detectives, sharks, Indians, and other things. Sometimes they take me for a walk with my dog Pepper. We often go to Central Park. I like going to the Wildlife Center there.

Grandma and Grandpa also invite me to their house for dinner. The food is great and we play detective. I love my grandparents. They have helped me a lot. — Ryan, 11

My grandparents do not play a big role in my life. They never talk to me. They ask me how I am but they don't listen.

I wish my grandparents would be a bigger part of my life so they could help me in reading and other subjects. I wish they would pay more attention to me by asking me how school is going and by listening to what is important to me.

— Amanda, 10

With the type of people my grandparents are, it has probably helped me that they weren't a large part of my life. You hear stories on how grandparents teach the grandkids about life and share their wisdom—yeah, right.

The only role any of my grandparents played was financial and I don't need that from family, I need closeness and love.

— Alison, 17

My grandparents, on either side of my family, have not played a very large role in my life at all. My grandparents on my mom's side were very abusive when my mother was a child and I hate them for it. There isn't even communication between my family and my grandpa. My grandma, on the other hand, we still see and speak to. She wasn't abusive like my grandpa. She just couldn't get out of the marriage or someone may have been killed. It could have been her or the kids. The only thing I could ever give my grandpa credit for is that I learned from him never to abuse anything or anyone. But, for what he put my mother, her sisters, and brothers through, I could never put in a single good word for him. He gives me the creeps.

— Girl, 16

My grandpa died before I was born. When I was old enough to understand that my grandpa was dead, I started to cry. I wish I knew him. My dad says that he was very nice. I see a lot of pictures of him. He looks very nice. My dad said that he hardly ever talked. I just wish that I could play with him. Sometimes, I wish I could go to the graveyard to talk to him alone. I would really like that. He just looks so lovable. I wish he was here. — Jeff, 10

I did learn something from my grandma. When my grandpa died, she never got over it. After he died, her life was wasted. She never did anything. She was always unhappy and she starved herself. From watching her, I found out that when you lose a loved one, you have to mourn but then get on with your life. — Rachel, 17

If there was one thing I learned from my grandma while I watched her on her deathbed, it was to be strong. I soon gained from my grandpa's knowledge after she was gone. He, too, was very strong. He would talk about her all the time and was not afraid of saying her name like some of us were. He taught me never to forget someone you love. — Troy, 17

When I was seven my grandma died. She was the only grandparent I ever really knew. What I remember of her, she was a beautiful woman. She was so caring and innocent. I remember my mother taking me up to her house to go fishing in her pontoon. When you entered her house you could smell sweet sugar and fresh coffee boiling for any unexpected company.

I never got a chance to say good-bye to Grandma. My mother thought I was too young to see her that way. I wish she wouldn't have done that. I may have been young but I was certainly old enough to say good-bye to someone I loved so much. — Nichole, 15

My grandmother has had a lasting influence on my life even though she died of cancer when I was four. I remember when I was three, she was sick and I'd sit on her lap and she would say, "A kiss is the best medicine." I would kiss her and feel important because I was giving her medicine to get better.

— Dafna, 11

Grandma would always babysit me. She was always there to help me. She loved me so much and I loved her as much. She was the greatest. She said I was the light of her life. I miss her.

— Brian, 10

■ ■ ■

I wish my Grandpa Charles had not died before I was born. He missed out on so much. — Charlie, 10

MARRIAGE AND
DIVORCE

**If your mom and dad divorce, don't worry. They just ran out
of love. — Breanne, 10**

ENORMOUS CHANGES HAVE occurred in the marital lives of millions
of Americans in recent decades. Divorce rates have soared and
remarriages abound. Families have been dismantled, shifted, and
blended in ways no one would have imagined not so many years
ago. In the middle of this upheaval live children who are deeply
affected by the marriages and divorces around them.

Some children write of their appreciation of households held
steady by loving marriages, others of their anguish as parents'
marriages crumble. They tell of envy toward peers blessed with
happily married parents and of the comfort they try to offer to
friends devastated by a disintegrating union. Some lie awake at
night wondering if their own parents' marriage will somehow
weaken and wither away. As they observe the relationships the
adults in their lives build and destroy, they form notions about
how marriage, and possibly divorce, will figure in their own futures.

Marriages fail, they say, for a whole host of reasons, among the
most common of which is that people get married too young and
for the wrong reasons. People leap into marriage because they're
infatuated, the sex is great, their friends get married, or they're

too insecure to live alone. Too often they marry because of an unexpected pregnancy.

Spouses abandon marriage because they're inconsiderate of one another's needs or too focused on career or material gain, say many. Several suggest that the divorce rate has risen because women have gained financial independence, and their husbands are feeling threatened. A fairly common notion among the kids is that in a busy, complicated society in which both spouses work, little or no time is spent nurturing the marriage.

Many kids blame disrespectful spouses for divorce—husbands or wives who nag, come home late or vegetate in front of the TV every evening. They see parents who fight too frequently or viciously or who are constantly critical of one another. Kids are very aware that financial problems, too, can tear at the marital fabric.

Alcohol and drug abuse, domestic violence, and extramarital affairs also lead to divorce, say kids. Scores describe watching their parents engage in physical violence. One says she once grabbed her mom's hand and dragged her into another room to escape a father hurling dresser drawers at her. Others tell of calling the police so someone will make their parents stop fighting.

In an age when divorce is socially acceptable, they say, there's little incentive to save a faltering marriage, especially when people have no religious orientation.

The youngsters sometimes present dispassionate accounts of divorce and its causes. But far more often they relate personal experiences that resound with pain and confusion. Children blame divorce for everything from their failing grades to their drug addiction. Hundreds link anger over divorce with the increase of violence among young people. A fourth-grade girl who was beaten up by a classmate explained his behavior this way: "His parents had decided to get divorced and he had to decide who to live with." Although it is widely known how important it is to tell kids that divorce is not their fault, youngsters commonly write about their struggle to believe that they truly aren't to blame. Kids from divorced families frequently express a far deeper heartache than kids writing about a parent who has died, especially when a divorce means one of the parents, usually the father, abandons them.

All the essays about divorce aren't bleak. Some children tell of their healing over time or of how the end of an abusive marriage improved their lives. The trauma of divorce is considerably lessened for those children whose parents maintain a civil relationship and focus on what is best for the children. It is especially helpful when fathers maintain a constant presence in their children's lives. Many youngsters describe with great joy and delight the weddings of parents who remarry. The lucky ones say that a divorce and the consequent remarriages of their parents have given them a larger family to love and be loved by.

What keeps a marriage together, according to the kids, is commitment and a willingness to work hard and remain faithful for a lifetime. Spouses stay married when they don't yell at each other and instead call each other every day to say, "I love you." "The most important point in marriage is love and romance," writes Melissa, 10. "People usually always like to have a little romance and tender love once in a while. It seems to make people feel really happy and warm inside."

Despite the possibility of divorce, most kids do want to be married one day because they want security, children, and the joy they truly believe marriage can offer. "I will get married," writes Bridget, 9, "because I think if I don't get married, I won't really live a whole life." Many believe life without marriage would be unbearably lonely.

For some, marriage is primarily a utilitarian proposition—they want someone to help clean the house and pay the bills. One 11-year-old boy requires of his future spouse that she be good at picking out carpeting, tiling, and furniture.

The qualities they expect in a spouse vary enormously depending upon their taste for blondes or brunettes, baseball players or lawyers. One of the most common qualities they require is kindness. As one elementary-age boy writes, "People who are kind to each other stay married." Another very common criterion is that their spouse be their best friend—open, honest, fun, and affectionate. Melinda, 11, writes, "Your spouse should be happy and have a sense of humor. He or she should have a joke for you when you need one." Some have very specific requests: a girl born in June, for instance. They want a partner who doesn't love her job more than her spouse, a woman with pretty legs, a great kisser, a person who won't fall apart in a crisis. Some say they will only marry someone who has never been married before.

When young people write about marriage they cover enormous amounts of territory based on what they observe in the media and in their own lives and the lives of people they know. But whether they're writing about marital sex or extramarital affairs, abuse and delusions, of marriages that flourish for a lifetime or end in divorce, most of their writing conveys a sense of hope—the hope that one day they will enjoy a sustained and sustaining marriage.

■ ■ ■

I want someone who would have a nice personality and someone who is pregnant so we can have kids. — Boy, 9

I will get married to someone I would like to spend a lot of time with. She will be nice, funny, like sports, have a job, be a good cook, and like pizza. I hope she's like my mom.

— Matt, 7

I plan to get married. I look for good looks, stylish clothing, good sense of humor, intelligence, kindness, and good manners. She also has to like General Motors cars. — Michael, 12

I'd like my wife to be willing to have a whole bunch of babies—even to have quadruplets a couple of times.

— Benjamin, 6

My wife would have blond hair and green eyes. She'd be funny but serious sometimes. She'd be smart, pretty and nice. We would go to parties once a month and go to baseball games. We would especially have fun. She'd give me a kiss every day and love me. She'd listen when I talk. She would brag about me a little. We would spend ten minutes talking to each other each day. We would have three children, Bobby, Amy, and Rick. She would be my best friend. — Boy, 11

The qualities I would look for in choosing a spouse are gentleness, kindness, no bad language, wants children, knows when beaten, doesn't drink or smoke, and most of all, doesn't have AIDS. — Jessie, 8

When I get older, I'm going to carefully select a husband by looking for things in people like patience when other people are using the bathroom. — Laura, 11

In my husband, I will look for someone who can and will do his own laundry. — Beth, 10

The important part is that I won't marry a guy who drinks, goes out every night, comes home later smelling of ladies' perfume, and his clothes are messed up. — Girl, 11

I would look for a spouse that was very nice, honest, and would let me get a dog. — Mike, 9

Love, support, and caring can help a marriage stay together. Two people need to talk about everything and support each other. They should grow with each other day after day, closer and closer. No matter what happens to a married couple in love, they can make it if they have a true relationship and marriage.

I am getting married this June. I'm getting married because I want to and I love my fiancé very much. We understand each other. We support each other about every little thing that goes on in our lives. We grow closer and closer every day whether we are together or not. We care for each other and are happy and content. That makes us want to be together forever.

I would look for a spouse who is loving, caring, supportive, responsible, giving, truthful, and sincere. He has to be there for me when I need him. I have found all of that in my fiancé.

— Heather, 17

I want to get married because, mainly, I'm afraid of being alone. I need someone to be there for me, like a safety net, if anything goes wrong. — Gail, 12

If I'm a semi driver, I won't get married. If I'm not a semi driver, then I will get married. — Boy, 11

I am going to get married so each night when I come home from work I'll have someone to talk to and visit. Also, I'll have someone to miss when I'm on business trips. — David, 10

■ ■ ■

I don't want to be married. I think it would cost too much and I hate girls. — David, 10

I don't want to get married because then the kissy stuff happens. — Boy, 8

I don't want to get married because with the career I'm planning a wife wouldn't fit into my life. Besides, what if a wife doesn't like to move around, and that's what a baseball player does! What if I got traded? She wouldn't want to leave her friends just to move to a new town. If all this happened we would probably start to fight and end up in divorce. I don't want to bring anyone into this at all. — Brian, 11

I am not going to get married. I'd rather live by myself. I don't want to get married because girls have much different tastes than boys. One reason is, if I get married, my house may get all decorated with bows. — Joshua, 11

In the old days, when women would get fed up with men, they would just sit there and take it. Now we divorce them.
I really can't say if I'm going to get married. Now I think no way would I marry. I want to make a wonderful medicine. I want to be the best scientist there is, and find the cure to cancer,

and be on the cover of *Time* magazine. I don't think I would have time to be married.

I have a twin sister to share secrets with. I would like a bulldog to scare away robbers, instead of a man. It wouldn't ever argue with me. I would be the boss. — Tara, 12

■ ■ ■

The hardest part about growing up is having to deal with all of my own personal problems along with my parents' marital problems. It's not fair. Why do I have to deal with my parents' problems? — Boy, 16

It's hard for me to listen to them fight. It makes me feel real sad so I try to make me feel happy by going to watch TV or listen to the radio or just sit still and think. It works sometimes and others, I just take the pain. The next day it would mostly go away. Then I'm just happy it's gone. — Girl, 12

When we were young and fought, adults separated us. Now adults are separating. Childish, isn't it? — Girl, 15

Over the years it has become more and more acceptable to get a divorce. Now kids my age plan to get married twice— once for money and once for love. — Nathan, 15

Divorce means a certain kind of hate for someone you were or are married to. — Girl, 9

■ ■ ■

Almost every one of my friends' moms and dads are divorced. It's like a disease or something. — Jesse, 11

I think that more people are getting divorced these days because everybody is getting greedy. So, when a man or a woman sees something else he/she likes better, they leave what they used to have and try to get what they want now.

— Boy, 11

The reason for so many divorces these days is that people all want their own way. Nobody is willing to compromise as much as they should. Marriage is just a big tradition thing. Maybe if everyone is getting divorced, the tradition should just get dropped. — Jill, 15

I think people get divorced because they maybe got married in early age and turned into a whole different person when they grew up. — Girl, 8

■ ■ ■

Most of the time people get divorced because of alcohol, drugs, and their bedroom manners. — Kyle, 11

In most divorces, the problem seems to be directly caused by over-closeness. They tend to smother each other and not let each other grow in their own special way. The reason that this ruins marriages is the fact that we feel like caged animals. And who would a caged animal attack if it could? Its capturer, of course. — Bruce, 17

I think the divorce rate has increased ever since women's lib has taken effect. Ever since women started working more and more, and staying home less and less, the male ego has been threatened. Fewer males are getting married because they aren't mature enough to handle the competition. If men do "take the plunge," it's because they think they're big enough to handle it.

But, surprise, surprise. The minute the woman starts making more money than the man, the man runs to some stupid blonde so he can finally be smarter and more successful than someone, which causes the marriage to end in divorce.

I'm still undecided about marriage. We'll see if men get more mature in the future. — Angie, 14

Maybe people get divorced because they want some peace and quiet. — Riley, 9

To get a divorce, you have to go to court. My brother and I had to sit on the benches. It was not fun. — Girl, 9

The one good thing about my father's death was never having to worry about divorce. — Kathleen, 13

I remember when my parents told my brother and I they were getting divorced. It was a year and a half ago and my dad sat my brother and me down on the couch. My dad said, "I care about and respect your mom but I don't love her anymore."

"I don't understand how, after twenty years, you can just stop loving Mom," I said as tears filled my eyes. I looked at my mom who was sitting in the corner crying and I wondered how he could put her through such pain.

Slowly, I started to feel a sense of hate towards my dad. I tried my hardest to persuade him to change his mind. "No matter how hard you try to get rid of me, I will always be your dad," he said as he started to cry.

I had never seen my dad cry before. It made my brother and I more confused. I thought my parents were a perfect couple but I guess there is not a perfect couple and nobody knows the real reason for divorce. Because if my dad stopped loving my mom after twenty years, there is really no explanation for anything. — Girl, 17

I love my mom and dad very much even though they don't hear it a lot, but I do, and I know I always will no matter what happens between them. You can't just stop loving your parents because they are divorced. That has nothing to do with it. — Jackie, 14

When my parents got divorced, I couldn't understand why. In my parents' case, the divorce occurred because of another woman. I couldn't imagine that my own father lied to my mom and me for so long.

The way my parents got divorced has got me worried about getting married. I don't think I'll settle down until I'm thirty–thirty-five years old. I don't think I could be faithful for so long and I don't want to inflict that much pain on my spouse. — Boy, 15

For six months after the divorce, my little brother was in his own little world. He didn't want any contact with anyone in the family. He moped around the house like a sad little puppy dog. Whenever I looked at him, he just glared at me with hatred in his eyes. Whenever my mom asked him to do his chores, he just yelled at her and punched her with a tight fist until her arm was all red. He banged his head against his wall until he had a big lump on his head. At night, he didn't want anyone around because he felt like no one wanted him around. He was afraid for a week and a half because he had the idea of being hurt again. He felt like a big tight knot, because of all the anger he was experiencing. When my dad had finished packing and was on his way out the door, my brother clung to his leg and screamed bloody murder for half of an hour until his face was red as a beet. Two hours later he sat in a corner with his face as white as a sheet because he feared that he would never see my father for the rest of his life. — Girl, 17

A couple of years ago my mother and my stepfather got a divorce for one reason and one reason only: He tried to kill her. He still torments us, sometimes, but we just try to live with it. I will tell you, though, it's not easy living when you jump at just a dog barking or a neighbor's car door slamming at night. Some people ask me what I would do if he ever came over again. I think I would *kill* him, maybe. — Girl, 12

When I was little I used to throw things at my sister like scissors and hammers and I started that after my mom and dad had fights. Because my dad used to throw glass plates, glasses, and other glass things right at my mom when he got very mad and he would drink. When they were fighting, me and my sister would scream. And that's how I got violent. — Girl, 12

The husband shouldn't throw the wife on the ground.
— Boy, 11

In the last year I've learned that when my parents fight, it's not my fault. When my parents divorced there is nothing I could have done to make them stay together. I could not have done better in school or helped out more at home. — Kari, 14

I was happiest when I still had a family! I don't have a real family anymore because my parents got a divorce not too long ago! Well, my heart is now in two and I can never fix that.
— Girl, 10

I was happiest when my father sat down the family to tell us him and mom were getting a divorce because I was sick of listening to them fight day and night. It was hard to listen to them because I was only seven and I didn't want to go through life remembering all that stuff that was going on between them.
Now I'm nine and they're still not divorced and I listen to them fight all the time. Their divorce will be final next month. Then that's when I'll be the happiest. — Girl, 9

Some people think having four parents is weird, but I actually prefer it. — Rebecca, 13

The most blissful time in my life was when my mom and dad got married—for the second time. This was the most blissful time because I love my mom and dad so very much. When they were divorced, I was so lonesome for my dad that I went nuts! When they were divorced, it was hard for me to stand that they were. When they wed, I was so happy that when we got home from church I was running around and I drove my mom up the wall. I made my dad go nuts. So he sent me to my room to settle down.

I went to my room and thanked the Lord. — Rebecca, 10

My mom and dad are happily married with five children. Once my dad went on a business trip that lasted for a week. During that week, we missed him a lot, especially my mom. One night she even called him at 1:00 in the morning and talked to him for at least an hour. I think this is part of what makes my family so close. I feel I am very lucky to have such a loving family. — Carin, 11

The thing that keeps a marriage together is to get the person mad before you marry them so you know what their bad side is. — Dan, 10

I think I will get married. You see, my parents weren't married so I would like to see what it is like. — Girl, 11

I think I have a very good chance of getting married because I am almost a straight-A student. — Jim, 10

■ ■ ■

I think I am going to have a good marriage when I grow up because I'm going to be real picky. — Kira, 11

I know every marriage can't work, but I sure wish they did.
— Ehrin, 11

OTHER KIDS

POPULARITY

Of course there are popular people that are nice. However, they are small in numbers and there are none where I live.

— Zach, 12

ASK AN ADULT to recall junior high and high school and most will readily remember their position on the popularity poll. Ask them to recollect their classmates and they probably can just as readily recall who belonged to the "in crowd," who was deemed a loser, and who occupied the middle ground. Most adults remember very well those days of glory or humiliation during which they were judged by their peers as to their social acceptability. Today that popularity game continues to be played just as relentlessly by many kids and the results of their efforts remain the same as those in years past—a mix of the exhilaration of acceptance and the pain of rejection. When writing about their feelings on popularity, some kids tell of years spent trying to conform to someone else's vague notion of cool and of pillows damp with tears when they failed. Others tell of the benefits of being ordained popular—lots of fun, good times, and the confidence that comes from being liked and emulated.

The primary requirements for popularity these days are looks and money. Popular students are adorned in the latest fashions with all the correct labels. They sport hairdos that owe their lives to gel, mousse, and spray. Their jeans are appropriately torn, rolled, or pinned; their shirts tucked in just right or left to flow coolly in the breeze. The girls are most often blonde and thin, the boys athletic and muscular. They possess the look, the walk, the attitude. "Coolness" oozes from everything they say and do.

To acquire the accoutrements of cool requires a lot of money, so parental status often figures into the popularity scene. It helps to have a parent who drives a flashy car, is employed in a high-profile profession, and lives in a swell house replete with VCRs, Nintendo, computers, and party rooms.

The youngest kids, the first- through fourth-graders, offer sweet views of popularity. Popular kids in those grades can wiggle their ears or will share their lunch. The popular boys tell funny jokes, the popular girls have perfect penmanship and are nice to everyone. Sometimes it's the cut-ups, the class clowns, the mouthy kids who put on a show who attain popularity; other times it's the studious, pleasant youngster, kind and conscientious.

In about fifth grade, suddenly the competition is on for boyfriends and girlfriends, for trendy clothes and lots of attention. The intensity seems to peak through the middle grades and then subsides in the last years of high school as kids decide to ignore the game or play by their own rules.

Many writers' recountings steam with bitterness and snide remarks. They say kids become popular because they're phony, devious, back stabbing, shallow, and will do anything to achieve status. Mean, snobby, and snotty are frequent descriptions of members of the "in crowd" who outsiders say spread vicious rumors, betray friends, and hit, kick, and put down anyone who doesn't meet their standards.

"When you're popular you get the freedom to tease and laugh at unpopular kids," writes Pam, 11. "It's very important to be popular because otherwise you get stepped on by popular kids and you get a low expectation of yourself."

Even some of the kids who describe themselves as popular say they're ashamed they treat other kids so poorly, but they don't want to jeopardize their position with the popular crowd. One 13-year-old writes, "I think popularity and judging people is wrong, but I'm not strong enough to fight against it. If I stand up for what I think is right, I'm scared of becoming a 'nerd.' "

Most recognize that some kids are popular because they are nice, confident, successful people who don't become self-centered or vicious. These kids are loyal to their own friends, but still remain friendly and kind to those outside their particular group.

In some schools the popular are divided into the glamorous group consisting of the good-looking, fashionable, and too often stuck-up kids; the respected group who participate in extra-curricular activities, are friendly and destined for success; and the harder-edged rebels who openly flout convention and loudly disrupt school activities. The value of academic achievement varies by school. In some, straight A's confer instant "nerddom." Several kids say they've watched their intelligent friends deliberately blowing tests and lowering their grades for the sake of remaining popular. But in other schools, academic achievement is admired. In virtually all schools, athletic success ensures popularity.

Drinking and smoking are necessary for popularity in some crowds. One teen writes that he was the designated driver at a Halloween party at his house. He took thirteen kids home and says, "Eleven of the kids I took home were drunk and didn't know how they got home. I feel pretty good about being popular."

Those identifying themselves as popular describe its benefits as having lots of friends to talk to, getting an enviable number of party invitations, always being included in whatever fun is occurring, and having a better chance of winning school elections and contests. Some suggest popularity is particularly important in the early teen years when young people are pulling away from parents and turning to their peers for advice and consolation.

Yet becoming and staying popular can become a kind of job. It's hard work to figure out what the codes are, dress fashionably, get the hairstyle to work, and learn the language and the expectations. Then, to stay popular, students have to make sure they never mistakenly talk to a nerd, disagree with the group leader, or do anything that could be perceived as uncool. "It is hard work to be popular," writes Kristen, 13. "You have to re-prove yourself to everybody daily."

The anger, hurt, and bitterness felt by those who don't achieve popularity explode from many young people's responses. Those labeled geek, nerd, dweeb, jerk, or retard suffer through watching friends abandon them and even participate in their mortification. They worry about being bullied and tire of the public psychological beatings. They spend hours in front of the mirror trying to figure out what it is they're lacking. They tell of buying expensive clothes and flaunting their possessions hoping that will somehow turn the tide. They even on occasion try to buy acceptance by proffering gifts. Their writing rings of the loneliness of the rejected and the confusion of people who never seem to fit. "Around school I'm called a dog, a dinosaur, and they even say I'd crack a mirror if I looked in one," writes a 12-year-old girl. "I wish you bullies, cool dudes, and straight-A students would see it our way."

Most kids locate themselves somewhere between the popular and unpopular crowds and declare that's the safest and most comfortable place to be. There they can have true friendships and reveal themselves as the people they are. Existing in the middle means they don't have the pressure to be perfect and that they can freely associate with kids either "above" or "below" them without worrying too much about their reputations. But even those in the middle get irritated by the favoritism sometimes shown to popular kids by adults. Rory, 12, writes, "When I was younger, I didn't really care who was popular. Now I do because they get the leading roles in plays and never sit on the bench in sports."

Eventually most kids seem to learn that true friendship is the most valuable and that being yourself, whether that means being hip and cool or dweebish, is the best policy. Yet as Tim, 15, writes, "It seems to me that kids are always going to be lumped into two groups. Some are always going to be well-liked and some are not. It's too bad that life can't be perfect and everyone could be the same."

■ ■ ■

What makes kids popular is stuff like not wearing hats in the winter. — Todd, 11

If you have twelve friends, you are popular. — Talia, 6

To be popular you need to have a lot of friends and to be a cute girl. Do good in school and get a good report card. Do all your work and don't have to stay after school. Don't think you are so cool. Dress well, not like you're a person who smokes.
— Katie, 7

You cannot be popular if you are ugly or fat, even if you're the nicest person in the world. — Melinda, 12

■ ■ ■

Popular kids get popular because they play sports, have more friends, and they aren't from a different country such as Korea like me. — Eric, 11

What makes kids popular is when their mom gets married to a rich guy. All their kids get to be popular in school.
— Heidi Jo, 11

What makes someone popular? Popularity can be summed up in one word—*excitement!!!* There are two types of excitement, positive and negative.

Kids who are positively exciting can be good-looking, athletic, and smart. They wear cool clothes and have neat possessions that other kids don't have. These kids hang out with other popular kids and date the coolest guys.

Kids who are exciting in a negative way are daring and reckless. They like the attention they get for breaking the rules. They may take drugs, smoke, or drink alcohol just because it's forbidden.

These two groups are quite different, but people are attracted to them for the same reason—people find them exciting. — Corin, 10

To get popular you have to punch someone out in school. Who cares if you get in trouble? Hey, you're popular.

— Zach, 10

If you go out every night and get smashed, it is more than likely that you will be popular. (That is, if you have the right wardrobe to go along with it.) — Girl, 15

Sometimes kids sacrifice their sense of what is right and what is wrong in order to be popular. For example, a student in a class may look in the teacher's answer book for the answers to a test and then tell the other students the answers so that he will be popular. — Michael, 10

Some kids try so hard to be popular they even do other kids' homework when they don't have their own done.

— Gretchen, 12

■ ■ ■

Very few kids are popular for kindness. — Mike, 10

Popularity is putting people down and walking around with attitude. Everybody thinks that's cool. I should know. I used to be the one acting cool and putting people down until my dad sat me on his knee and got it through my thick skull that popularity doesn't come from acting cool or walking around with a bad attitude. It comes from inside. The people who think acting cool is cool are very wrong. — Joel, 11

Most of the girls I know that are so-called popular can spread gossip or rumors faster than a speeding bullet. That's why they're popular—they have the power of mouth and no one dares to go against them. — Brena, 15

It was different when we were little because then being popular meant who had the best toys or the strongest dad.

— Tiffany, 11

She walks into school with an air of assurance about her. She is tall, with long blonde hair and an exceptional figure for someone only thirteen. She has a clear complexion, wears just the right amount of makeup, and has on an outfit that is one of the latest trends. She belongs to the most prestigious clique in the entire school. In fact, she started it herself.

She knows how to get what she wants, when she wants it. She appears to be an honest, hardworking girl, but underneath she is clearly a deceptive person. She is the future prom queen and captain of the cheerleaders. She has been placed on a pedestal, high above everyone's reach.

Every school has at least one of her. They are powerful, very powerful. They have so many followers that it's almost sickening. Why, I ask, do these people control so many while being so insincere and superficial?

Many people deny the fact that popularity is important to them. They'll say over and over again how it's not the good looks and the cool clothes, it's the person's true personality that counts. *Ha ha!!* I laugh at that statement! As if anyone truly, I mean deep down, believes that. — Raina, 13

In our school almost all of the popular kids are really good in sports. I hang around with the so-called "popular kids." I am good in sports so I feel I fit right in.

Popularity has been important to me. It kept me out of as much trouble as I could have gotten into. I feel it has kept my grades from falling in the pit. I'm not sure if that's how my parents feel, but that is how I feel.

As I have been getting older, I feel more popular and I feel that helps me. I am short, so sometimes I get teased, but I really don't mind. I feel popularity has made my life, up to now, a whole lot easier. — Mike, 13

It is important for me to be popular because I like attention and if I was a nerd everyone would ignore me or beat me up. Beating up isn't the kind of attention I like. — Chris, 12

If you are popular you never walk in the halls alone, or have to sit alone at lunch or have no one talk to you during free time in certain classes. The people who aren't popular think those who are "in" are snobs and idiots. This is not so. Most of the time the unpopular kids are afraid of being declined friendship. They keep away from popular kids and make fun of them because *they* are afraid. My feelings haven't changed about being popular because it is just a fact of life. If you are popular, great. If not, maybe just ask a popular person for advice.

— Mike, 13

Popular kids don't have to worry about forgetting their lunch because other kids will give them anything they want.

— Willie, 11

■ ■ ■

I don't think all kids want to be popular. Just the majority of the unpopular ones. — Kristina, 11

Why? This is the question I ask myself every morning when I look in the mirror. It's just not fair how some people have everything when others have none. As I put on my makeup I try to cover up the way I feel. It's hard. My dad always says, "Put on a smile and you will be popular. Put on a smile and you will have friends." Is this true? I'm running out of smiles.

Friends and popularity must be some of the hardest things teenagers face, unless you're one of the lucky ones. Will I ever be one of the lucky ones? Will I ever mean something to this world? Or will I just end up in the pile of nobodies who have been brushed aside from all the rest?

The words "It's not fair" still ring in my head as I leave for the bus. Maybe tomorrow will be better.

My dad has often tried to comfort me. It helps for a while, but then I start thinking again. I really don't know how parents could help. Maybe if they just keep on loving us, we'll pull through ourselves. — Angie, 13

I used to be best friends with a popular girl. When she became more popular, she started acting mean and very stuck up. When she met more kids that acted like her, she didn't like me anymore. — Amanda, 12

If a girl likes a popular guy, and he's out of reach, she'll go after his friend as a stepping stone to the popular guy.

— Matt, 15

All of the popular kids go through girlfriends or boyfriends like disposable pens. — Brian, 12

To some people popularity is the most important thing in their lives. These are the people who usually don't last at the top for very long because they are so worried about being popular that they forget to be nice. — Jason, 14

■ ■ ■

Being popular is like being a king. Everyone is always following you around. It can be a real pain sometimes.

— James, 11

It isn't important to me to be popular because popular kids have girls following them. It's like the boys have remote controls so the girls will follow them. I would not like girls following me around. — Jeff, 9

I don't want to be popular because people will bug me. You don't get any privacy, you're busy all the time. You get phone calls day and night. It gets aggravating and maddening. You can't get any time alone or with friends. I wouldn't want to be popular at all. It is a bunch of trouble. — Jeremy, 9

When you are not popular you can make mistakes. When you are popular, you can't make mistakes. — Brion, 11

I don't really care or want to become popular; there are too many pressures and ideas to live up to. One girl killed herself in this area recently and she was quite popular. The popularity was too much for her. She couldn't handle it, so she took the hard way out. — Marisa, 13

When I started out in school it was rough for me. No one liked me because I was the friend of a girl who had Down's syndrome. It means she's a slow learner. I always thought I was a failure. Nothing was going right for me, but my friend was more important to me than being popular.

As the years went by, my friend and I grew apart. I love her, but it seems as if I grew up and she didn't. I'm sort of popular now, but not stuck up. I would never want to hurt my friend's feelings, but I'm afraid I am. I know what it feels like to be an outcast. I also know what it feels like to be popular. When it comes to being popular or keeping the best friend you've had for almost seven years, which would you choose? — Karna, 12

Popularity can be a dangerous thing; you tend to forget about your real friends. Then when you lose your popularity, you don't have any friends and you are left alone. — Nathan, 11

I don't really care if I'm popular because I never have been and I'm used to it. I think being a nerd is better sometimes because then any friends you have are your true friends.

— Jessica, 13

■ ■ ■

The ones who care about me and the rest of the world are the ones who I count as popular. I just wish I didn't have so many fingers left over when I finish counting. — Aimee, 16

It isn't very important to me to be popular because I have other things to do and think about. I just need enough friends to make it through life. — Katie, 13

It doesn't matter if you're popular because your mom and dad will still like you. — Paul, 9

PEER PRESSURE

Peer pressure is like being in a cage with a lion. If you make one wrong move, you are dead meat. — Joseph, 12

AMONG THE STRONGEST influences on children are their friends and peers. Friendship is vitally important to their happiness for the same reasons it is for adults—comfort, acceptance, and love. Young people frequently write sweet essays describing the friends they love, real and imaginary, and the friends they lose. For some, their peers are more important than family. But while their peers frequently give children joy, they also give something else—a dose of pressure so strong that many kids write down "peer pressure" as "pure pressure."

Youngsters relate tale after tale about making decisions based solely upon the opinions and pressure tactics of their classmates and friends. Their submission is rooted in one of the most basic human needs—to be accepted by the community. Most admit that they will change hairstyles or buy clothes they don't even like for the sake of belonging. Others make decisions on which classes to take, which sports to try out for, which parties to attend, and which classmates to consider acceptable all on the basis of their peers' views.

Some say they cave in to their peers' suggestions or demands because they truly respect their friends' opinions—that's why they're friends in the first place. Others admit they follow along because of their own insecurity. Some actually believe that their friends and associates know more than they do and are inherently better people. For most, the degree of peer influence is directly related to their self-confidence, and for many youngsters struggling to develop their own sense of worth, self-confidence either is lacking or very fragile.

Many capitulate because they're actively threatened. "Peers can be so powerful because if you don't do what they want you to do they call you a wimp and spread it around that you're a nobody," writes Emily, 12. They're told if they don't buy a particular blouse, their "friend" will tell everyone what lousy fashion sense they have; if they don't shun the person the group has decided to shun, then they'll be made fun of and kicked out of the group; if they don't accept the dare to break a window, they'll be called a chicken by "everyone"; if they don't smoke the joint as it's passed around, they'll be considered babies.

Many young people say they feel terrible after they treat someone else cruelly, and swear it won't happen again, but when another situation arises, most still find themselves being persuaded to engage in behavior or adopt attitudes with which they disagree.

According to many young people, one reason for the power of peer pressure is that children rarely have meaningful conversations with parents about the pressing issues in their lives, in part because their parents are rarely home. So some kids, especially teens, turn to their peers as a surrogate family.

That peer pressure also has a positive side is acknowledged by many young people. For example, peer pressure can challenge a timid child to do a physical or social act requiring courage. There's positive pressure when a young person runs with a crowd opposed to the use of alcohol and drugs or in favor of academic achievement and accomplishment. One girl, 17, writes, "Right now I'm trying to be drug- and alcohol-free all over again and peer pressure from my friends is helping keep my life straight. When the desire for a drink or the desire to use drugs comes along, I call a friend or two and talk about it. Even though they seem to be bawling me out, they are just showing that they care."

Many kids can rattle off the "correct" approaches to handling negative peer pressure. Just say no. If a friend wants you to do something against your will or better judgment, he's not a friend. Have the courage of your convictions. The problem is that many admit they cannot transform the abstractions into real life behavior; it's too hard when they're face to face with friends determined to make them comply with the group. However, over the years, kids generally discover a cadre of friends with whom they share similar values, making them less susceptible to the negative pressure of others. Some point out, however, that peer pressure exists in some form throughout everyone's life.

The young writers' views vary widely on what adults can do to help. Some say adults should simply allow their children to learn the difficult lessons on their own, but a common view is that parents and other adults can help in one basic way—by building their children's self-confidence, the best defense against peer pressure. Parents, they say, need to tell children that they're loved and be specific about the ways their children are unique and special.

One unlikely but appealing solution is suggested by Michelle, 13. She writes, "The only way for peer pressure to end is if young people themselves change. If they remember how uncomfortable peer pressure was for them, maybe they'll stop pressuring others."

■ ■ ■

Peer pressure is very strong for me. When I was about seven, I was pressured to get to the top of the jungle gym. The jungle gym was the biggest one I had ever seen. The kids who were pressuring me were older than I was. I felt that if I didn't do it, they would call me names. I got to the top and was very scared. My mom came and got me down.

When peers take over your mind, it's like you're the robot and they have the remote controller to control you with.

— Jenny, 11

I make decisions depending on what my friends say. For instance, how I dress. I always ask them, "Is this okay?" or

"Are you sure my hair looks all right?" Being a girl, it is important for me to fit in and have people like me. — Jane, 11

I almost never make decisions by myself. I usually follow my peers' decisions because I am not a good decision maker.

Sometimes to make decisions I walk over to our neighbor's fence and if the dog barks within ten seconds, the answer is yes. If ten seconds is over before the dog barks, the answer is no. — Jesse, 11

It seems like when I make all of my worst mistakes is when all of my friends are around. — Troy, 16

Peer pressure is something that doesn't let me be myself. Once when my friends and I were making up a dance to the song, "Lollipop," my two friends thought of a step that I didn't think belonged in that dance. I was afraid to speak up and disagree even though I didn't like the idea. One of the girls is really popular and I was too afraid to speak up.

— Heather, 11

A lot of times I wear clothes that are not the warmest but are what my friends are wearing. I would like to dress warmer because it is cold outside. Even my mother tells me I will be cold if I do not wear them. I know that she is right but I want to dress like them because I do not want them to make fun of me. — Amy, 13

Peer pressure affects everyone in different ways. I've sometimes made decisions just to go along with others so I wouldn't be left out. For instance, I went to the movies with some friends and they were drinking a wine cooler, nothing big but something definitely wrong to me. They kept on asking and bugging me to drink some so I finally did. I just took one drink but I knew I shouldn't have been so easily pressured. I think I did it mostly to prove I could and so I wouldn't be called chicken. It's scary to be left out. You don't know what to do. I learned a lot that night and I think that we kids should be able to say "No" no matter what. If it had been more than a wine cooler, and more than one drink, or even something more dangerous, I might not be writing this. I'm glad I said no after one drink.

— Amos, 13

I've experienced peer pressure. I hate it. I get it especially from guys. They want sex all the time. If you don't give it to them, you're a zero. — Girl, 14

I think that your own opinion is sometimes less powerful than your friend's opinion. A person is never fully secure with their own opinion because inside of us all there is a feeling of insecurity and failure. — Joshua, 14

Sometimes the pressure gets so heavy you feel like you're going to explode. They pressure you to do things that they think are right for you or for them. You're not sure if it's right for you. Deep inside, I don't think that your friends are sure either. They just guess. — Andrea, 12

No one is innocent. We all have felt this social pressure and have exerted it ourselves. I am not free from this. I have done and have said things I am not proud of because I would have been rejected if I didn't. The sad part is that I'm sure my actions influenced others who were struggling with the same crisis when they saw me surrender and conform. — JeRay, 17

I was walking with some of my friends when they decided to tease someone. We called this person names and made fun of what he looked like. I didn't say anything because if I did, I thought they would make fun of me. After we teased him, I left. I felt terrible. I told my friends that I had a headache. After

I thought about what I had done, I felt that I should say, "I'm sorry" to this person, but I never did. Maybe next time, I'll be able to walk away when my friends start teasing someone. I hope so. — Scott, 11

Peer pressure is something everyone has to deal with. I remember one time, in the summer after fourth grade, I was at my friend's house and we decided to make a swing. This swing was made out of rope, a potato sack, and two big trees in her front yard. She decided that I was going first, and being in fourth grade, I was very insecure, so I went first. Well, the swing broke while I was in the air and I landed on my head and got a concussion. The only two things I could remember were my name and what my dad's car looked like. Since then, I've pretty much done what I've felt I *wanted* to do.

— Beth, 13

Generally, I do not make decisions on the basis of what my friends think. I try to do what is right without my friends' help. Because I choose to do this, I am sometimes left out, ignored, and alone. But still I am content. I am content because I have no fear of getting into trouble and I am happy about myself.

— Joseph, 10

I used to make a lot of my decisions based on other people's opinions and not my own. However, I wasn't any more popular or well-liked than I am now. I was just more unhappy.

— Darla, 14

I try to be myself and to act the way that I want to act and to wear the kind of clothes that I want to wear. In short, to be original.

Just look at my wardrobe—every piece represents something about me. I own some very dressy clothes, but mostly my wardrobe consists of casual, wild things because that's the way

I am. I've been known to wear tennis shoes with a long black skirt, a fishing hat with a denim shirt and a miniskirt, white leggings and a polka-dot bubble skirt.

Sometimes kids laugh about my "weird" clothes, but I don't really care. I get a kick out of seeing my friends' reactions to what I wear and I think my friends like me because I am myself and I don't try to imitate anyone.

So if you're worried about being a part of the "in" group, there's really no reason to be. If you're truly yourself, your friends will like you even more—and you'll earn the title "leader," not "follower." — Sue, 14

If you try too hard to impress other people and make all your decisions based on what they think, then you're not living for yourself and eventually you forget who you really are.

— Dawn, 11

When you get older you learn that your friends now will probably not be your friends when you are forty years old, so you have to start making decisions based on what you think not what other people think. — Jon, 16

I think one way we could get rid of peer pressure is to have everybody look, talk, and act the same way. But then, life would be very boring because there would be no originality at all.

— Mike, 11

If you really want to be a friend to someone, let them have their own ideas. Don't tell them how to act or what to do. You might like them better if they're not you. — Tracy, 12

■ ■ ■

Adults can't really do anything about peer pressure because kids care more what other kids say than what adults say.
— Shelli, 15

Most parents and other adults don't really believe that peer pressure exists. They think it's just an excuse for immature behavior. — Shannan, 13

I feel that I can honestly say that I almost always make my own decisions. I am my own person with my own values and I can do what I want. If my friends and I are shopping and they want to go into a certain store and I don't want to go there, I will tell them to meet me somewhere and I'll go where I want to go.

The reason I'm so independent and can make my own decisions is because my parents allow me to make them. They don't make my decisions for me. They give me input on what they feel is right, but I make the ultimate decision. If I make a decision and they think it's wrong they will let me know how they feel but that's it. That is how I learn. — Tiffany, 14

To help with peer pressure, adults should encourage kids and help build up their self-image. Adults should also learn to be trustworthy. Encouragement is most powerful when it comes from someone we trust and respect. When someone we respect stops to tell us that they're proud of us or we're doing something right, it helps to build self-confidence, and maybe the next time we're in a touchy situation with peer pressure, we'll do what we believe is right again. — Mary, 16

I think that adults should let their kids handle it. They should only intervene if their children are in danger or if they are asked to help. — Mike, 14

I don't think adults can stop peer pressure because a parent can't go up to a friend and say, "Stop pressuring my kid."

— Andrea, 12

Someone in school will suggest that you join in a rule-breaking activity. Usually a valid response would be, "No, I'm afraid we'd be caught." This could have been used a few years ago, but it's no longer valid. Every streetwise kid knows that you probably won't be caught. This lack of discipline in the school system gives peer pressure room to grow.

— Nathan, 15

Sometimes pressure is really hard to handle. I think pressure slowly kills a person's confidence. I think a very good way to handle peer pressure is to talk to friends, family, pets, or even God! — Amy, 13

■ ■ ■

If only everybody would be themselves, we wouldn't have these problems, but who will be the first to volunteer?

— Luke, 13

THE DIFFERENCE BETWEEN
BOYS AND GIRLS

Boys care more about girls' looks and girls care more about boys' feelings. — Amy, 7

FOR SEVERAL DECADES American society has struggled with the question of whether or not boys and girls are inherently different. Experts have proposed that boys play with dolls to develop their nurturing side and girls play with "boys' toys" to become more aggressive. Today's girls are encouraged to play sports and excel at math while boys are supposedly encouraged to be more emotionally expressive. Parents read articles and books searching for hints on how to raise their sons and daughters as equals; teachers examine their methods and materials for sexism; researchers keep striving for answers to all the gender questions.

But what really has changed? Apparently not much, for most kids continue to describe girls and boys as if they were two separate species.

Generally they say boys are rough, rowdy, daring, aggressive, cruel, macho braggarts who revel in fighting, belching, and making rude noises with their armpits. They rarely cry and are careless about other people's feelings. They delight in "gross" things, love to laugh, and are quick to slug those who offend them. Girls, in general, are described as gentle, nice, neat, giggly, goodie-goodies. They care enormously about their appearance and treat a broken fingernail as a major trauma. They are disgusted by crudeness and intensely fearful of rodents and bugs. They live to shop, fall in love frequently, and spend their hours gabbing and gossiping with their friends.

Both girls and boys believe that girls reveal their feelings more easily and are more sensitive to the effects their words and actions have on others. Some believe that boys actually don't feel the same things the same way, including Robin, 13, who writes, "When a loved one dies, most girls cry whereas boys sit there thinking about sports." Others, however, believe that boys experience the same emotions as girls, but are unable or unwilling to express them. A boy, 15, writes, "When I lost one of my grandmothers in a car accident, I could not cry, but my cousin who is a girl cried her eyes out. It's not like she loved her any more than I did, it was just that I couldn't bring my feelings to the surface."

Boys are more honest than girls, say many; for instance, boys will be direct, even rude, in their criticism of someone's clothes. Girls, instead, will pretend to like something, then trash it behind the other person's back. A few believe boys, being less concerned with rumors and reputations, have far more freedom in expressing their views than girls do. It is also thought that boys keep secrets better.

Looks are a girl's first priority, say many. Girls diet constantly, worry about their hair, spend hours in the bathroom applying makeup, and are never satisfied with the results. Boys accept their physical selves far more readily and appear to be less influenced by media images of the perfect body, face, and wardrobe.

Friends play an important role in all young people's lives, but girls tend to have close friends while boys have buddies to play sports with, tease, and tell jokes to. "Girls give their friends a hug to show their respect, but boys punch each other and say, 'See you tomorrow, ya loser.' It means the exact same thing," writes Ben, 13. One teenage boy writes about the problem with this attitude: "When you want to talk, your friends think you're kidding around."

Another striking difference between boys' and girls' friendships is the volatility of girls' relationships. From about age nine to fourteen, girls frequently write about nasty feuds with friends, often over seemingly trivial events. The boys, by contrast, rarely describe the cattiness, jealousy, and lingering hurt feelings of the girls. On the rare occasions where they are openly upset with a friend, boys are more likely to engage in a fistfight, after which things return to normal. In the long run, though, this stage in girls' friendships seems to have a positive result. High school girls are far more likely to describe deep, intimate friendships than high school boys. It's as if the early years spent feuding teach the girls how to relate more deeply and give them an appreciation of true friendship.

A common view is that boys have better self-images than girls and rarely diminish themselves or their accomplishments. While boys brag easily and often about their greatness, girls instead frequently put themselves down. For girls, their self-esteem appears to be rooted in what others think of them. They're more likely to follow rules and stay out of trouble for fear of displeasing someone.

When kids write about their futures, girls are increasingly likely to aspire to careers once considered traditionally male. Yet when explaining their common beliefs that there will never be a woman president, both genders say women are too emotional, not smart enough, and not good leaders.

One disturbing trend showing up only in recent years is that girls are becoming more like boys in their tendency to use violence, especially against other girls. Among elementary-age girls, the change means they're more likely to punch someone on the playground rather than engage in verbal warfare or tears. For teens, the source of the violence is usually jealousy over boyfriends. A fifteen-year-old accosted by a classmate jealous of her boyfriend writes, "I was walking across this park, she came up to me and asked if I was who I am, and if I was going out with this guy, my boyfriend. When I answered yes, she nailed me. In retaliation, I hit her back and ended up winning the fight. Kids my age are very morbid. When people heard what happened, they asked me why I didn't finish her off."

Accounts of violence between boyfriends and girlfriends also are increasing. One teen writes about how she responded to her boyfriend's beatings in kind, until he cut her neck with a knife and she called the police. A sixteen-year-old writes this: "I've only used violence once to try to resolve something. My boyfriend broke up with me and I was crushed. He hurt me so bad I wanted to kill him, but I didn't. I developed such a hate for him that I beat him senseless, and he's twice my size. I felt pretty good afterwards. Actually, I felt so good that if I could turn back time, I'd do it again."

Attitudes toward gender are changing in confusing and sometimes unexpected ways, but one perception about girls and boys that will always ring true regardless of the era is that offered by Jena, 14: "There might be a lot of differences between girls and boys, but there's at least one thing we all have in common. We all need love."

■ ■ ■

Boys and girls are different because girls like the smell of flowers. Boys don't. Boys like worms. Girls don't. Girls like having slumber parties. Boys don't. — Isaac, 9

Boys usually go out in the world and do things while girls stay in the house and knit and sew. Boys go hunting, hiking, fishing, and biking. Girls stay inside and do quiet things like play dolls and house and read about what boys do. It seems that girls live longer so it seems to pay off that they stay inside and do quiet things. — Joe, 9

Girls like arts that you draw because they can use their imagination and boys like clay because they can make a mess.

— Natasha, 11

Boys and girls are in general half and half. I'm a boy with a twin sister. She likes to knit, cross-stitch, and be by girls a lot. I like to take things apart, kill bugs, and run my model train so fast it goes off the track. We both like to rollerskate, ice skate, watch TV, and have snowball fights.

So, in general, boys and girls are fifty-fifty. — John, 10

Boys and girls are very different. For instance, if a girl came up to a lion, tiger, or bear she might say, "Oh, look at the cute lion, tiger, or bear." But if a boy came up to a lion, tiger, or bear he might say, "Look at the ugly lion, tiger, or bear. I think I'll shoot it!" — David, 9

■ ■ ■

Boys like to kill little animals and insects, like mice and spiders. I've never had an urge to kill a mouse and I don't know a girl who has. Girls don't like to see things die. I've never seen a girl say, "Want to see a spider's guts?" while squashing a spider. — Kim, 10

■ ■ ■

When girls get to the mall, they go into a weird trance. They want to buy everything. — Mike, 11

Parents say girls are smarter. Girls say boys are rough. Boys say girls are too quiet. Teachers say they're equal. Parents say boys aren't responsible.

I say it's a hard decision.

Girls say boys are weird. Boys say girls are dumb. Parents say girls are polite. Teachers say boys are little gentlemen. Teachers say girls are little ladies.

I don't know what to say.

Girls say boys aren't cooperative. Boys say girls don't know anything. Mothers say girls are cute. Fathers say boys are cool. Parents fight over the subject. Boys and girls argue, too.

I wish this was over.

Boys say girls don't know how to play sports. Girls say boys can't jump rope. Parents have had it with both of them.

I think this is a mess! — Brian, 11

Girls and boys are different. The boys on the bus run up and down the aisles while the girls read. The boys do dumb things in class while the girls sit and listen. The boys fall backwards in their chairs and I've only seen one girl do that. The boys don't do their reading work. They push people down on the playground. Boys don't even know how to do cartwheels.

— Auda, 8

There's one or more boys in my class that act very young and unintelligent. Like the boy that sits in front of me and the boy that sits in back of me. Also, the ones on both sides of me.

— Girl, 10

The world has to face it: Boys are just immature. — Girl, 12

We girls go to a dance to find guys, to dance and have fun, not to watch our male classmates tear down the decorations and play tag on the dance floor. I wonder if we'll ever be on the same wavelength or if they will always be children to us.

— Lynn, 15

Most often good students are girls. Good boy students must have become extinct or something. — Boy, 13

Most girls would like to go to places like France, Paris, and Italy. Usually boys are happy with going to the lake to catch fish or frogs. — Megan, 10

Have you ever thought about what it would be like to wear a bra? It wouldn't be fun! If you're a guy, try putting a belt around your chest and buckle it behind your back. Now, walk around like that all day. Trust me, you wouldn't like it; I tried it. — Boy, 15

■ ■ ■

Girls always have a sensitive way of saying something. When they say something they say something nice. Boys, they can talk nice, but only when they're in love. — Tanya, 9

An example of girls' politeness is that no matter how much they hate the school lunch, they always say "thank you" to the cooks. — Kristin, 10

Girls are funny. When they lose they cry. Instead of working harder, they give up. — Ryan, 12

Boys feel that they can't cry, so they act more cruel toward others to hide their feelings. — Jennifer, 9

■ ■ ■

Guys take sadness and turn it to anger. — Gwen, 15

It's harder for boys to apologize because then they have to admit they were wrong. Boys tend to laugh things off because a lot of times laughing is easier than crying. — Kara, 13

When girls get hurt they usually feel bad. Every time boys get hurt they get up and pretend nothing happened so they don't ruin their image. I think they feel like crying, too.

— Deandra, 10

If a girl hugs a girl, you think nothing of it. If a guy hugs a guy we start getting strange images in our minds. — Boy, 14

Boys appear to be very tough and hard and girls appear to be meek and mild, but deep down inside each might not be what they appear to be. — Girl, 10

Guys are more direct with their emotions. If two guys have a disagreement, they will argue about it openly. Two girls having an argument tell all of their other friends and write notes to the person they are mad at, but they will very rarely confront the person they have a disagreement with. — Matt, 13

Boys get blamed for anything, like if both a boy and a girl break a window, the boy would get punished. — Boy, 10

Boys tease girls when they see them playing with their Barbie dolls, but then they go play with their G.I. Joes. I've got news for you guys, G.I. Joe guys are dolls, too!!! — Andrea, 12

Boys get their kicks out of teasing and aggravating girls, especially sisters. Have you ever seen two boys laugh so hard about calling their sister a name that they get to the point of breathlessness? If not, you haven't met my brothers.

A few weeks ago my brothers started putting me down because I told them our car doesn't have a carburetor. Then they tested my car knowledge. It was so hard explaining the different parts when they'd yell, "Wrong!" before I even said anything. I actually do know a little about automobiles (and our car does not have a carburetor), but would they listen? No!

My point is that boys feel self-confident when they are able to put someone down and their conscience doesn't nag them about it. That's one way boys and girls are different. Girls are really aware of that little voice in their heads saying, "That was wrong. That was wrong. That was wrong." Teasing someone triggers that voice and girls cannot handle the guilt. That's why girls don't tease as much.

Furthermore, teasing takes up time we could be using to do our hair. — Amy, 13

Boys can be easier to talk to because they don't blab everything you tell them to their friends. I think it's harder to talk to someone of your own sex because they will tell their friends about what you said. They know better than the other sex what will hit soft spots so they tease about that. People of the other sex are easier to talk to because they can't usually know what will hit hard so they're usually content to listen to you and let you get it out of your system. Then when you're through, they give you sympathy. — Sara, 11

Guys don't have to worry about their reputations very much at all. It's so much easier for them to be cool. They can do pretty much whatever they want and no one really cares. Girls, on the other hand, have to think about what they do and say all the time. As soon as girls do or say something, it's all over the school. — Laura, 14

■ ■ ■

There are a lot more boy nerds than girl nerds. — Kevin, 11

Boys will laugh at a funny joke. Girls will laugh at something that someone is wearing. — Josh, 11

Girls seem to be more "fakey" in front of their peers while boys pretty much act themselves. This is very apparent when one compares how each answers a phone. When a girl answers, no matter what sort of mood she may be in, it is usually in a happy, high-pitched voice. When a boy answers, it may sound like "Yo" or "Hey" in a low-pitched kind of grunt.

If a girl hears some sort of gossip that is *never* supposed to be told, it will eventually be told to everyone and spread around the entire school. If a boy may hear gossip, he'll most likely reply with a "So?" and leave the entire matter alone.

— Alicia, 15

Boys sometimes hide their hurt, tears, and fright for fear of damage to their reputations. Girls sometimes act scared or dumb or don't speak up with what they want to say just so they don't seem braver, smarter, or more in command than the boys. — Shelly, 13

A girl's way of saying that she thinks she's smart is, "I'm so stupid," and everyone responds, "No, you're not!" She already knows this, but it is a way of getting compliments nevertheless. Boys, on the other hand, say what they think or would like themselves or others to think. Using the same example a boy would say, "I'm smart" and his friend answers, "I'm smarter" and thus, a competition arises. — Erika, 12

Women all try to be dainty and petite, but really they are all pigs. Working at a Dairy Queen I see this quite often. Women come in with their boyfriends and their mouth says, "Small fry and small diet," but their face says, "Give me everything and make it a large." — Jeremy, 14

When I'm with a guy, I eat as little as possible so he won't think I'm a big eater. Guys don't care and eat what they want.
— Girl, 16

■ ■ ■

Girls take small bites of their food. Boys inhale their food, then let out a good belch and say, "Whoa, did ya hear that?"
— Boy, 15

Men and women think different. Women think they're smarter than men and some men believe it. But why do men have all the good important jobs like lawyers, presidents, senators, judges, builders, and sports? These jobs all take a lot of thinking. Girls seem to be smarter in school, but in real life, men are. — Douglas, 14

A teenaged boy usually drops out of school and that makes girls smarter. That is why lots of men's jobs don't need smarts.
— Girl, 10

Men farm and ladies do not. Ladies cook and do housecleaning. Men do not. Most of the time girls use umbrellas. Boys usually do not use umbrellas. — Jay, 9

There are some tomboys that live in my neighborhood. They play football with you, they play baseball with you, even hockey. When we play football she is just like one of the guys. She hits you as hard as you hit your friends. She can run as fast and throw as good. Then the day comes when she starts to get good-looking and she doesn't play because her friends don't approve of it. It's better for both her and us.

— Noah, 14

Boys and girls are identical mentally. If a girl is brought up like a boy or if a boy is brought up like a girl they both act the way that they were taught. Take Tarzan, he was raised like an ape so he acted like an ape. — Erik, 11

One day in gym we were playing flag football and our teacher was passing out flags. The girls didn't get flags. When they asked why, the teacher said, "When the boys grab for the girls' flags they scream, so I'm not giving the girls any." This is an example of how teachers sometimes treat boys and girls differently. — Chris, 13

Boys and girls are very different from each other because we teach them to be different. Boys are taught to feel shame and girls are taught to feel they can't do anything. People are constantly telling boys that if they do something not "manly" enough, that they are a sissy. And they're telling girls that if they play contact sports, they are not "feminine." Maybe someday they will start teaching girls and boys to be "people," to be whatever they want to be. — Lindsay, 11

INSIDE
ME

SELF-IMAGE

I think I like myself because I am loved so much.

— Rory, 10

WHEN KIDS WRITE about their families or friends, their beliefs or opinions, they often reveal how they feel about themselves as well. No matter whether they're first-graders or seniors in high school, they're forming their self-images and experimenting with expressing their unique selves to the world. Sometimes they find their self-discovery exhilarating, other times terrifying.

For the younger kids, describing a favorite facet of themselves is relatively easy. They rattle off attributes from being kind to doing great cartwheels to being able to rescue distraught kittens from trees. They're proud when they learn their multiplication tables and take great delight in making someone laugh or in conquering their fear of the dark. One says his best accomplishment is that he can pronounce all of the ingredients on a food package. Others describe unabashedly how smart they are in school and what awesome baseball players they are. The boys and girls both exude an excitement about shaping their own character and identifying their possibilities.

Older kids, though, wrestle with the question about what's best about themselves, particularly teenage girls who admit they find it far simpler to enumerate their flaws than their strengths and to sing other people's praises instead of their own. Katy, 16, writes, "Most teenage girls feel like they're not good enough for this world. You feel like you're not pretty enough or smart enough. If you don't have every guy after you, or even one, there goes your self-esteem." Unlike the younger kids, teenage girls are less likely to reflect on their accomplishments and struggle instead to define themselves in terms of their relationships with others—they're a good friend, for instance; they listen well, they're nice to people. Teenage boys tend to focus on their actions and physical accomplishments, their athletic, academic, or mechanical abilities, for instance.

For most kids, it's much easier to tell what they'd like to change about themselves than to talk about what they like.

A surprisingly large proportion of kids say they are too shy, including Lisa, 13, who writes, "I let my shyness creep over me like an itchy blanket that I want to throw off, but that I know I'll freeze without." Many youngsters and teens admit they're terrified of expressing their true opinions in a group for fear that they'll be seen as abnormal or weird. Frequently they berate themselves for pretending to be what they aren't. As Lizzy, 12, puts it: "You may be angry, but you act happy. You may be smart, but you act dumb. You may be childish, but you act mature. You like someone, but you pretend you don't. We seem to put on masks to cover up our real selves."

Far more girls than boys say they want to improve their self-esteem. They frequently depict themselves as pushovers or phonies. They also readily accuse themselves of being overly sensitive, too moody, and too quick to cry. Many girls say they would like to be more outgoing, including Trisha, 14, who writes, "I usually keep most of my feelings to myself and after a while people quit asking me how I feel, so nobody knows but me." Ironically, many girls who do describe themselves as outgoing and outspoken say they'd be better off toning themselves down; people, they say, seem to prefer girls who are nice, quiet, and unaggressive.

Boys, too, are concerned about their self-images, but they are far more likely to evaluate their sense of humor and level of self-confidence. While many girls deplore their inability to express honest opinions, some boys are bothered by their inability to express honest emotion. Boys also admit to being too reluctant to admit to others that they have a problem. James, a senior, writes, "I would change my ability to deal with serious problems, instead of burying them someplace in my head. This place is my graveyard for all bad things that have happened to me, safe from anyone trying to exhume the thought."

"To be smarter" is a common refrain from girls and boys of all ages who believe that better grades would secure them more friends, better futures, and happier parents.

What they like and don't like about themselves often derive from the same source—the reactions and words of parents and peers. Among the most damaging influences on children's self-esteem is the cruel teasing they inflict on one another. Their feelings are hurt by kids who taunt them for things they can't control—their looks, their race, their circumstances. They can be teased because their mother is in a wheelchair or because they have eczema or asthma, because they wear glasses or suffer from a learning disability. But peers can also be great bolsterers of one another when they accept their friends for who they are, compliment one another's efforts, and treat one another with understanding and respect.

The deepest damage to children's self-esteem, kids say, can be done by parents. Kids frequently write about how inadequate they feel because their parents constantly criticize or mock them or give them too little recognition for their accomplishments or their qualities.

But parents also can be children's greatest source for good feelings about themselves. Their parents' praise and encouragement allows them to develop a solid center that can withstand assaults by their peers or the world.

At the core of children's self-esteem is the basic question, "Am I worthy of being loved?" Most of them believe, and all of them hope, the answer is "yes," because as Erin, 14, writes, "You can survive anything, even growing up, if you are loved."

■ ■ ■

The best thing about myself is that I'm honest and caring. You're probably wondering if this is true. It's true. I asked my best friend about it. — Michelle, 9

■ ■ ■

The best thing about me is that I like to eat. I will eat almost anything you serve me. — Joshua, 6

My best quality is being curious. I've learned many things, and have become interested in many things by being curious. My room wouldn't have all the nine planets painted on the ceiling if I hadn't been curious about astronomy. Curiosity got me interested in geography. It got me interested in computers, too. We now have a computer and I enjoy it more than if I hadn't been curious.

Sometimes it's not easy being curious because some people don't like it when you ask questions. Maybe they don't know the answer or it takes up their time. Curiosity has made my life special, that's why it's my best quality. — Jesse, 10

I am a creative person, which at times can be hard because the world we live in is dominated by logic and reason. For a creative person, self-esteem is hard to keep up—so often we are not rewarded.

Reality is all that matters and those who think differently are rejected or ignored in their lifetimes. And those creative individuals who are recognized, are honored posthumously. I don't want to wait that long.

If we don't reward those individuals who see things differently, like myself, nothing of great value will ever be created.
— Scott, 13

I would like to be braver so I could eat more foods like squid, tentacles, liver, octopus, and snake. — Ricky, 11

I would change my imagination because sometimes it gets out of hand. For example, I think my stuffed animals are alive.
— Colin, 8

I look in the mirror and think of all my friends who are so much prettier than me. I always wonder if boys like them better than me. I often compare my looks to my friends' looks. I guess I shouldn't do that, but I always do. — Girl, 14

■ ■ ■

I'd like to have more power. . . . I do have power, but since I'm small, everyone takes it away from me. — Kristin, 10

I would change my personality because when I try to be funny, nobody laughs, but when I'm not trying to be funny, everybody laughs. My goal is to be funnier than my grandpa.
— Shane, 10

I'm always too aggressive. This little problem seems to get the best of me. Oftentimes when I get into discussion groups, I will take over the discussion without a second thought. This trait takes away almost any chance at making really good friends. Not being able to make good friends scares me.

Ever since I was little, I was in sports and activities that usually needed aggressiveness. Mental toughness was drilled into me and I learned fast that being passive got me nowhere. Making friends has always been very hard for me, but I try very hard to soften myself so I can get to know people.
— Matt, 18

I would learn to be more patient. I miss all of the surprises because I have to open my beautifully wrapped presents with the shiny bows right away. I wish I could just sit down and hold them, trying to guess what is in it by feeling it. I could shake it to see if it rattled. Instead, I tear it open right away. The surprise is over and done. — Mary, 11

I wish I could be a singer. I like to sing. But every time I try to sing, it always comes out like a big blob of words. Then my parents come by and say, "What is all that racket?" I go, "I was trying to sing again, Mom." Then my parents started to giggle and then they started to laugh even harder. I asked what was so funny. They said, "Nothing."

I ran back into my room and slammed the door and started to cry. They came in and apologized to me and I accepted the apology. — Pam, 9

If I could change something about me, it would definitely be *how I act!* I want to act cool. I want to be like a funny guy so everyone would like to be around me. Sometimes it seems like nobody likes me and I'm dying inside. I try not to show it, but sometimes I can't and I cry myself to sleep and tell myself, "Don't worry, Brendt. Tomorrow you will act real cool!"

— Brendt, 10

I would change the fact that I am shy because being shy makes it easy for people to call me a nerd, although no one ever says it to my face. I know they call me one because out on the playground I overhear people say it. And it hurts to be called a name.

I have already made my change on the inside, but it is only seen by those who see me for who I am, not who I seem to be. And it is those few people who become my friends, and those few people who stick with me through thick and thin. So actually I have changed my shyness. It's just that no one takes the time to listen or to see the change. — Darla, 11

I would change the fact that I am easily embarrassed; therefore, I am too quiet. When I was little, teachers would refer to me as "the girl in the back row who doesn't say much, but always has a smile on her face." People used to say I was the teacher's pet because I never talked out of turn and was never in trouble. Even now I neglect to ask or answer questions in class when the room becomes silent.

Just once I would like to be called "the girl who always has

a devilish look on her face and an idea brewing in her head."
Just once I'd like to be sent to the library for talking too much.
But that would be too embarrassing! — Ellie, 14

I would try to get better at baseball. I want to change myself
so I won't miss so many ground balls and pop-ups. I would
change this by practicing every day through rain, snow, sleet,
mist, and even hail if it's not too big. — Michael, 10

I wish I could be smarter. Sure, I'm the kind who gets mostly
B's, but I wish I'd get A's because my sister and brother do
and they always make me feel like a loner. . . . I feel like I'm
not part of the family because I don't get A's.

If I want to change, I have to study hard and take my time.
Then I would feel much more welcome and I wouldn't have to
try and get my mom to like me better than my brother and
sister. — Katy, 10

I would change my ego and self-esteem. Before I was raped,
I was really outgoing and if I wanted something done, I would
do it. But after it happened, my ego and self-esteem went
downhill. I didn't like to be around people. I wanted to stay
by myself. I buried myself in a little hole. No one knew what
I was feeling and a lot of friends drew away because they didn't
want to hurt me more.

The only way I can get my ego and self-esteem back is by
forgetting what happened, trying to put it behind me and get
on with my life. It is going to be a long time for me to get back
to my normal self, but it's worth the wait. I can't give up because
I want to be my fun, outgoing self again. — Girl, 17

I wish I could be more positive toward people and have a
better outlook on life instead of checking out suicide books and
having low self-esteem. I always think about death. I think

about a lot of ways to kill myself, but something always makes me stop.

I don't like to think about this, but I can't escape these feelings. Sometimes I wonder what the world would be like if I killed myself. My parents would be pleased because there would be one less kid to take care of. I think I need to go to a psychiatrist to help me figure out what my life is all about.

Sometimes I think about my future and if I will know enough things to get a job. I think that a question will come up that I don't know how to answer and I will be forced to sleep on the streets. Sometimes I feel so bad, I want to cry. Some days are good and I don't think about this as much.

Sometimes my parents seem like they just don't want to listen to me, like I come home from school having a great day and I start telling them and they don't listen. I start feeling bad and I start thinking about it again. I come really close to killing myself. — Boy, 12

■ ■ ■

It hurts the most when someone says that you are no good and you can't play with the other kids. When they say that, I feel like going to Mars and blowing up the world. — Boy, 10

Never call your kid a name like dumb or any other unkind comment about how they act. I say this because once in a while it happens to me. When it does happen to me, my mom or dad usually say they are sorry, but even if they do, it still hurts me for a while inside. — Girl, 10

■ ■ ■

I could have been the one to discover America and my parents would say that I could have discovered Canada, too, if I "applied myself." — Girl, 17

Walking down the crowded halls of the school, I say to myself, "Don't let those idiots get to you today, Dandi!! Just ignore them!"

But when the teasing comes, I know that I can't handle being called those horrifying names. You know the ones I'm talking about, don't you? Butterball, Fatty Kathy, or my personal favorites, Blubber and Fatso. I live my life being humiliated by all those ignorant people out there who think that just because you're overweight you haven't got any room in that fat body of yours for any feelings.

I may be hurt for five minutes or so, but I bounce right back because I know that there's something seriously wrong with you if you have to call people names. Are you trying to show people that you're tough? Or are you trying to see how many people you can make feel awful in one day? — Dandi, 15

My feelings were really hurt when I heard someone talking about me behind my back. One day after my feelings were hurt very badly, I went to physical education. We did headstands and it helped a bit! So from now on, if my feelings are hurt, I just stand on my head! — Katie, 9

■ ■ ■

What hurts me most is not the things others say to me. It's what I say to myself. I have this malicious little voice in my head that tells me, "I can't." — Steve, 17

The hardest thing is the pressure society puts on us to be its ideal. Somewhere deep inside we all feel that we must be tall, thin, smart, and beautiful. — Jill, 16

I have a puppy, a girlfriend, a nice family, nice friends, and zits. Everyone notices them, even my dog! — Dave, 10

The nicest thing someone could say about me truthfully is my braces don't look awful. People call me names because of my braces. If someone just said one thing nice about my braces, it would make me feel good. — Missy, 12

The nicest thing a person could say is I fit in. Because it seems that whenever I go to a slumber party, nobody pays any attention to me, sometimes it's like I'm not even there.

— Amber, 11

Probably the best thing someone could say to me is that I'm weird. This may not be a compliment to someone else. But being weird or strange makes me different from everyone else. I like that. And I never want to be like anyone else.

— Brian, 12

I have cancer, and I lost my hair from the chemotherapy treatments. Of all the nice things people have said to me the one that made me feel best would have to be when my best friend, Joel, said to me, "Adam, I don't care if you don't have any hair, you will always be my best friend!" I was feeling down about losing my hair, but after Joel said that, it made me feel great! — Adam, 12

■ ■ ■

The best thing anyone could ever say to me would be, "You're my best friend, and I don't mind if you have a pacemaker." That would be the best thing anyone could say to a fourth grader that has a pacemaker like me. — Nicholas, 10

The nicest thing anybody could truthfully say about me is "I love you." I would hope somebody in my family would say that truthfully to me pretty soon, like tonight. — Joey, 9

STRESS

I have stresses in schoolwork, playing an instrument, and just everyday things like wondering if the world will blow up.
— Mark, 12

STRESS. SAY THE word and most adults can spew a litany of stresses in their lives ranging from marital problems to frustrations at the workplace to economic, physical, and emotional duress. But not only adults are suffering from stress. Most children experience it, too, and often find it overwhelming.

"Another name for stress is parents," writes Lori, 15. Her view is a predominant one. Parents cause stress primarily by expecting too much, kids say—great grades, success at everything, never fighting with siblings, and always making their parents proud.

Lives crammed with activities cause stress for many kids who describe schedules brimming with piano lessons, Hebrew school, sports, 4-H, Girl Scouts, church groups, extracurricular activities, farm and household chores, and jobs. Many of the teens who say they're overloaded admit that it's by their choice. But large numbers of elementary-age kids frequently say they're overextended because of parents. One boy, 11, writes, "During the summer I get lots of stress from my parents—take basketball, take baseball, take tennis lessons, take, take, take! It really starts driving you up a wall!" The dilemma such demands can cause is illustrated by one nine-year-old girl who says that she is far too busy, but doesn't want to tell her parents for fear of displeasing them. Her plan is to tell an adult and then maybe that adult "can talk to my mom and dad and maybe then my mom and dad won't enroll me in so many things." One teacher told me of a six-year-old girl in an exclusive private school whose parents had her so overscheduled that she'd come to her piano lesson, lay her head down on the keyboard, and fall asleep.

Academic pressures affect most kids' stress levels regardless of the type of student. Youngsters in gifted and talented programs (who frequently refer to themselves as "GT" kids) describe the stress they feel never to fail. The average students feel the pressure of reams of homework and of working their hardest but receiving only average grades. In addition, many of them suffer from comparisons with their more academically successful classmates or siblings. For those with learning disabilities, the stress is not to get discouraged by slow progress and to weather the teasing they sometimes suffer from their peers.

"Ever since my mom and dad got divorced, I've had stress from head to toe," writes one youngster. It's not just divorce itself that stresses kids, but also the ongoing tension between their parents, the arguments over schedules and support checks and custody. They feel stress when parents force them to make a decision about which parent they will live with, especially when the parents live hundreds or thousands of miles apart. For some, even greater stress occurs when a parent remarries. Suddenly the children are coping with the finality of the divorce, a new parent in their lives, the resentment the unmarried parent might feel, new rules. It is especially stressful for those kids who are forced to act as intermediaries between parents or who must lie to Mom or Dad to keep the tension level manageable. In addition to the emotional causes of stress, many write of the stress caused by the logistics of maintaining life in two separate households—lugging toys, clothes, and homework between homes.

Teens write that they're under stress not only from families and academic demands, but also from jobs. Some maintain three part-time jobs in addition to full-time schooling. They're working until late at night and on weekends and find themselves worrying about car payments, insurance, college expenses, and their diminished social lives. Some are living on their own because of family difficulties and must work to survive. Others are pressured to seek work for reasons other than survival. One girl, 14, says she doesn't want to get a job because she wants to enjoy what little childhood she has left but her parents are insisting she find work.

American mobility causes enormous stress in children who are frequently uprooted from their communities and schools. They feel stress at leaving friends behind and at adjusting to new schedules, schools, and peers. Frequently their stress is exacerbated by the stress their parents are feeling.

Stress is keenly felt by the sixteen-year-old mother who is struggling to finish high school, edit the yearbook, take care of her baby, maintain relationships with her family, her fiancé, and her friends and find time for herself.

The problems of the world and of American society in particular increase the stress level for many young people. They are worried about crime, AIDS, and the possibility that they may one day be homeless. They feel stress when they watch news reports of war or have personal encounters with racism. In addition they experience stress from peers pressuring them to experiment with drinking, drugs, smoking, and sex.

Other stresses are caused by romantic disappointment, alcoholic and abusive parents, deaths of loved ones, and squabbles with friends. Many are stressed by difficult family circumstances such as coping with a mother suffering from depression or living with a mom who has recently married husband number three, and already she is talking about moving out.

Youngsters cope with stress in myriad ways. Younger kids tend to climb trees, furiously pedal their bicycles, hide in closets, scream into pillows, sob into a pet's fur, make funny faces in the mirror, or talk to Mom and Dad. Kids of all ages see counselors and psychiatrists; some kids just get very quiet and distant from everyone. Some teens admit to handling stress by reckless driving and speeding. A few meditate or turn to yoga or crystals for help. Several pre-teens describe their bouts with tension headaches or gastritis. They cope by popping aspirin and prescription medication and even sleeping pills. Several kids say they respond to stress by overeating.

What adults can do to help, according to the writers, depends on the age of the child and the particular stress. A couple of nine-year-olds tell how helpful it is to have a parent sit down with them and organize their time, to actually draw up a schedule and give hints for how to make it all work smoothly. Parents can evaluate the child's needs and watch for signs the child is struggling with too much pressure; they can then be willing to allow children to drop out of activities they find too stressful. Divorced parents can reduce the stress on their children by cooperating more and recognizing how painful their continual fighting is for their offspring.

Back rubs, relaxed conversations, and bowling excursions with parents also are highly recommended as stress busters. A couple suggest that schools offer classes on stress management. Among the most important stress reducers, however, is adults acknowledging that children can feel as much stress as adults. Most important, adults can reduce stress levels by often reassuring children through words and affection that they are loved for who they are.

Several express the same sentiment as John, 12, who writes, "One thing I know for sure is that you're going to have stress for the rest of your life, so you better get used to it." No doubt that's true, but perhaps adults could at least work to keep the stress levels more manageable for their children. By recognizing that children's stress is real and by responding to it with reassurance and sometimes intervention, adults may be able to give them a wonderful gift—more childhood time, time to simply enjoy themselves and the world around them.

■ ■ ■

Stress is when I feel like screaming. I get a headache and a tummy ache. I feel nervous and then get very tired. Sometimes I cry. I don't like this feeling. — Scott, 10

It's six A.M. Time to wake up. A chore in itself. Take a shower. Hurry now! You still have to get dressed, eat breakfast, and brush your teeth before you catch your bus. Don't forget to comb your hair! Remember your lunch money! Oh, no, you didn't finish last night's math! Quick! Finish those last two problems! Here comes the bus! Grab your coat! Run to the stop! Whew, just made it.

Finally in school. Better hurry up and get to your locker! The bell will ring in forty-five seconds! Quick, close it! Lock it up! Darn, you're late. You'd better not be late again or you'll get after-school detention.

Time for lunch. Quick, get a good place in line so you'll have time to eat. Don't stand around and talk, sit down! Eat your burger and fries, fast! Not much time left! Gulp down the rest of your shake!

School's out! Think you can relax now, huh? Forget it. Hurry up and finish your homework! Eat supper quick! Eat, eat, eat, eat! You're going to be late for soccer practice!

Back from soccer practice at nine o'clock. Better go to bed so you can get a good night's sleep. After all, you're going to wake up early tomorrow morning!

Repeat cycle, five days a week, from ages twelve to eighteen.

— Jim, 12

Sometimes when I'm very busy I want to fall asleep and never wake up. — Siri, 12

The worse kind of stress for me is the tension and pressure I feel at home. I usually stay out of my family's way by not participating in family activities or discussions. I retreat to my room and try to dream up fairy tales. My parents' stereotype of the perfect daughter is something I could never be. Their expectations are high and seldom do I reach them. I usually choose to give up because I think there's no point in trying.

— Girl, 14

My life is stressful because my family is always too busy. Mostly we are busy during the weekdays. We always talk about it, but never do anything about it. We always say we can't drop out of anything. — Girl, 9

Stress is scary because it seems like what you think is right is pulling at one of your arms and what other people think and expect of you is pulling at your other arm. Sometimes it's just hard to make the right decision. — Kari, 13

■ ■ ■

Kids have too much stress because sometimes adults want us to be just as responsible as them and take on adult responsibilities, and we are only kids. — Sarah, 12

I feel stress when I have to eat something I don't like.

— Jason, 8

I consider my life a little bit stressful because I'm always getting blamed for stuff I didn't do. Like whenever I get in a fight with my eight-year-old sister, she lies to my mom and my mom always believes her. It makes me feel like she doesn't care what I think. It puts a lot of stress on me to think that she doesn't care. — Girl, 12

■ ■ ■

The kind of stress some people have is called "Beauty Stress." You sit there all day worrying about how you look.

— Laura, 11

I have Tourette syndrome. It is a neurological disorder that makes me make noises and swear out loud. I mumble a lot and call girls names. I cope with it by taking medication and vitamins and I try to relax by listening to my radio at night. I ignore people who don't understand it and then I tell them about it.

How can adults help? They need to learn what causes my Tourette syndrome. — Matt, 12

Stress is like a stray dog that won't leave you alone. No matter what you do, it keeps following. It is pointless to avoid it, for it will track you down; it is not wise to harm it, for the dog will cause you more pain, and it is fruitless to ignore it, for it will just try harder to get attention.

Stay busy . . . buzz around like a bee . . . don't let problems catch up with you, they may hurt you. . . . This is one way I deal with stress. It doesn't help. No matter how fast I've run, the dog has always caught up. — Girl, 12

The stress in my life is that I'm going to be a father. I'm not ready to be a dad yet, but I have to deal with it, I guess. Just the fact of having a child at the age of fifteen makes my life stressful, considering I have so much I want to do and now I have a child to raise. Other than that, my life is pretty much stress-free. — Boy, 15

The stressful thing in my life is when my dad goes in an airplane. I feel like he is going to crash. I feel scared when he goes on an airplane. I think he is going to die. I love my dad.
— Andrea, 7

Much of the stress I have to deal with comes from an alcoholic father who makes life very difficult for me. You never know what type of mood he is in. About the only thing adults could do to make life less stressful is to listen. Also, my father should become a coffee drinker. — Boy, 16

The kind of stress I have is my parents not getting along. The stress is really a bad stress, it's like you want to run away. I feel bad when my parents fight because it feels like I made them get mad at each other. — Boy, 11

There are many things that are stressful in my life. One of the things is having two houses and four adults in my everyday life. That can be very hard and stressful especially when both houses have different rules and expectations!! It's also hard to have two sets of everything like clothes, tapes, books, magazines, makeup, and everything else.

— Kirsten, 11

I consider my life stressful but a lot of it is self-induced. I am the one who volunteers doing all the extras that I know I don't have time for. I'm the one who's in all the arts, sports, clubs, and committees. I'm the one who feels it's necessary to have the A+ instead of the mere A. I feel that in order to be a worthwhile person, I must always *be* the best, striving alone isn't enough. This is a lonely, empty feeling.

My father has instilled these values in me since day one. When I set what I considered an unattainable goal and went on to reach it, I felt proud. But as soon as he heard of it, the response was, "Why aren't you more like so and so? You can do better than that. It's not that big of a deal. . . ." And the effect of my father has caused me to become disillusioned, depressed, and let down with everything. It's easy to be in many activities. It's easy to be good in something. It's not easy to combine the two.

So I turned it around. I've become ambitious, independent, and determined to succeed—for myself.

I've learned a lot in the last few years, too much of it the hard way. I have learned that I have to put my well-being first. No matter how many achievements I've racked up, none of it will be worth it if I'm not around to enjoy the rest of my life. Not only are we the ones who have to look in the mirror every morning and ask, "Why am I doing this?" We are the ones who must live with the answer.

— Sheila, 16

What parents sometimes don't notice is that "overachievers" can still have problems. — Barbi, 15

It's kind of stressful for me when I work hard at something and then bring home a report card with a B in that spot. It seems like all my dad wants from me is straight A's! It kind of hurts inside to know that nobody cares how hard I try; just how many A's I get. I know my dad means well, he even tries to reward me each time I do better, but I don't want gifts or money. I just want him to tell me he's proud of me. I wish he'd let me be who I am, not some whiz kid that I'm not.

— Girl, 10

■ ■ ■

My life is not stressful. It's full of fun, happiness, joy. My mom and dad don't want a lot from me. They just want me to do the best I can. — Aaron, 9

Do you consider your life stressful? There are times I do and times I don't. To me, when my life is stressful I have bundles of homework, piano, violin, and have to be somewhere at four o'clock. When my life is not stressful, it is Saturday morning and I am lying on the couch watching cartoons. If your life is stressful, do what I do: Think of Saturday morning. — Britt, 9

I sometimes think that my life is stressful, but not all the time. When I feel my life is stressed I usually go up in my room and talk to my blanket and stuffed animals or I go outside and sit on the swing. The breeze outside and the chirp of the birds makes it feel and sound very peaceful. My mom comes upstairs and talks to me when I'm feeling blue. She always has the cure for the blues. — Karen, 9

I cope with my stress by just taking some deep breaths. Sometimes I feel like I just want my stomach cut open and all the butterflies taken out. — Girl, 10

When I come home from school I sometimes get headaches from working so hard at school. I have to do my jobs, a half-hour of piano, and my homework, too. And I'm on the bus for a half-hour! That gives me no time to get a break, and with my younger brother bothering me it seems impossible!

Sometimes I like to see my dog. She's a Saint Bernard and really cheers me up when she slobbers all over me and slops me with her tongue. She makes me laugh and looks so funny I forget all of the stress and I'm ready to go back to work.

— Christine, 9

The way I cope with stress is by going somewhere quiet and peaceful—like my closet. I go up to my room and into my closet, I lock myself in and I sit in my rocking chair and read books. Or I go outside and talk to my pigs. They always grunt or snort back at me when I say something. — Katie, 9

Unlike my mother who blows up yelling, I deal with my stress by crying my feelings out to someone or I lie down and think it over. One of my favorite ways to deal with my stress is to make up "story" solutions. In my mind I make up perfect solutions to what is stressing me. I know that my solutions will never happen, but they calm me and make me feel better.

— Cassandra, 12

When I get stress, I just tell my teacher I have to go to the bathroom, but I really sneak down to my locker and get a Tylenol. — Girl, 11

I go outside and go up in my treehouse to get over my stress.

— Nathan, 11

■ ■ ■

It is stressful when kids call me names. But I just pretend that they are in their underwear and that they look like nerds with their underwear up to their necks. — Ryan, 10

I am not quite sure how to explain this method of coping with stress, but it's kind of like making your mind look through binoculars. When you are using binoculars you can only see straight in front of you and everything else is blocked out. That is kind of how this coping method works. I block out everything except for the one thing I'm working on. I call this channeling my vision. In this way, I don't worry about the stressful problem. — Kristin, 12

I don't consider my life very stressful, but if I did have stress I would cope with it like this. I would ride my bike around the block. The reason I do that is because there is almost no sound. And also, I can think better with fresh air. After I ride my bike around the block, I always feel better. — Jeff, 9

Adults can make life less stressful by helping us realize when we get too busy. They can help us decide if we want to still do everything or if we should drop out of some things.

— Kathy, 9

My mom hugs me so I feel better when I'm stressed.

— Mike, 11

Adults could quit issuing so many orders and expecting so much from us kids. We try our best. There is so much work at school and at home. There isn't any time for being me.

— Bette Jo, 14

SEXUAL
AWAKENING

My mom always told me that you're old enough to have sex
when you can do it with the lights on, talk about it after, and
accept the responsibilities and consequences. — Girl, 17

CLOSE YOUR EYES and take yourself back to the days when you
were making your first sexual discoveries. The nights making out
in parked cars or in secluded fields, the necking at drive-ins, the
locker-room talk about getting to first base or second or third, the
late-night groping on your parents' sofa, your wedding night.

Now think of the children you know. They are experiencing their
own sexual awakenings in much the same fashion as you did, but
judging by their writing, critical differences exist. Today's kids are
exploring their sexuality at younger ages, with greater openness,
in an era when virginity is considered by many kids—and adults
—to be abnormal, and sex, with its possibility of AIDS, can be
deadly.

According to a survey released in early 1992 by the Centers for
Disease Control, more than half of American high school students
have had sexual intercourse. About forty percent of ninth-graders
(fourteen and fifteen years old) have had sex, nearly seventy-two
percent of seniors. To find out why the kids think this is happening,
we asked these questions:

What are the main reasons why many teenagers decide not to

wait to have sex until they're older? Are the reasons different for boys and girls? What is the right reason or age for a person to start having sex? What's the best approach adults can take in talking to children and teens about sexual issues?

Most of the students who responded were over fourteen, and many wrote anonymously. Their essays reveal a complex mosaic of sexual feelings, attitudes, and actions, but one common denominator is that sex occurs because of pressure:

Pressure from peers who brag about their sexual exploits, real or imagined, consider virginity (the "dreaded 'V' ") a mark of shame, bombard each other with questions and taunts; classmates who, as one puts it, are "in a race to see who can lose their virginity first."

Pressure from the pervasive images of sex in the media. Soap operas and prime-time TV that are nearly X-rated. Movies that show teen role models hopping from bed to bed without forethought or consequences. Talk shows rooted in sensationalism and sexual innuendo. Advertisements dripping with sexual imagery or promising "love" if you just call this 900 number now.

Pressure from the music they love so much with its Madonna videos, songs like "I Want Your Sex" or rap about being hooked on a hooker and having those "sex attacks."

Pressure from raging hormones and a society that pushes them to grow up fast. "Not only the teens are involved with sex," writes Mike, 16. "Most of the world revolves around sex."

Teens have sex, some say, because it relieves stress, offers escape, and can be a better high than drugs. They "do it" to feel mature and prove their manhood and their womanhood. They don't wait because, in a world of disease, war, and ecological disaster, they aren't sure how many tomorrows they have left. They engage in sex because they're "horny," curious, lonely, drunk, rebellious, in love.

Nicole, 16, writes, "Sometimes it isn't the child's hormones that cause him or her to behave the way they do, sometimes it's their hearts. Both parents usually work, leaving the children to themselves, and a lot of time work comes home with the parents. These parents don't realize they're neglecting their child, and if you told them so, they would probably deny it wholeheartedly." She's one of hundreds who suggests one reason teens have sex is because it's the only way they can get the attention and affection they crave.

Most say that while both sexes are pressured—boys most often by boys and girls by boys—in general they view sex differently. "The guy is thinking, 'If I give her love, she'll give me sex,' and the girl is thinking, 'If I give him sex, he'll give me love,'" writes Nicole, 16. Several say some girls have sex because of low self-esteem, while most boys have sex because of the pleasure and the "score." A few think that girls can be equally aggressive sexually, and frequently are. One girl writes, "Guys may feel that sex is the only way that they can show affection and receive it. Other types of affection for boys seems rather taboo."

Ironically, despite the pressure for both boys and girls to have sex, a double standard prevails. One of the most frequent themes is that it's acceptable for boys to have sex with as many girls as they like, and their reputations soar, but girls who have sex, unless it's with a long-time boyfriend, are whores. A few say some girls have figured out a way to cope with the dilemma—they have sex just once. That banishes the "V," but avoids the "slut" brand.

Alcohol is frequently a factor in sexual experiences, according to many. An eighteen-year-old writes that she had thought deeply about when she'd have sex, but then she got drunk at a party: "This guy was putting the moves on me, and I gave in after knowing him five hours. . . . If I hadn't been drinking I wouldn't have had sex with him because I had decided that I had to go out with a guy at least for four or five months before I did it. . . . My self-esteem has been dropping lower ever since, and I only see a slut when I look in the mirror."

Several suggest some girls have sex because they're forced into it. A seventeen-year-old boy writes, "For a junior the pressure is greatest to have sex. I would bet that most of the girls in my grade have had sex and probably with different people. People are going to parties at a younger age than before. At these parties the kids are drinking and the ones who can 'handle' it ask or take the smaller women and have sex with them."

The right time to have sex, most say, is that ambiguous time when you're "ready"—that is, you love the person, take precautions, and can accept the consequences of pregnancy and sexually transmitted diseases. Many say that time can't be measured in years, but others recommend distinct ages before which sex should be avoided, usually fifteen or sixteen. The late teens and early twenties also are frequently cited as appropriate times to engage in sex.

A substantial minority says that marriage is one good reason to have sex, but few see it as the only reason, and even fewer view sex as a sacrament. Teens see little reason to wait in an era in which people marry later, are likely to get divorced, and in which premarital and extramarital sex is commonplace among adults.

What do they want to be told about sex? Everything. They want straightforward conversation—not lectures, accusations, or denunciations—that covers both the physical and emotional aspects of becoming sexually active. Most say they want more of that information from parents, but almost never get it and when they do, it's frequently too little too late. What they want most is the truth about how their parents feel and what they know. One of the worst things adults can do, according to one, is to pretend to be naive. Unlike past generations, in which kids often didn't realize their own parents have sex, today's kids are fully aware that the adults in their lives are sexually active. For instance, many are aware that their divorced parents frequently sleep with people to whom they're not married.

In spite of their awareness and supposed sophistication, scores acknowledge that the subject can be embarrassing and difficult. But if parents won't inform them, they say, they'll find out elsewhere or engage in sex with insufficient knowledge. The conversations should begin around age ten or twelve or even earlier, or it could be too late, many believe. Those who offer opinions about sex education generally favor it, but they say they need better-trained teachers, more openness, and a willingness to tackle the tougher aspects of the subject. Only a couple believe sex education encourages kids to be sexually active.

Despite their requests for open and loving discussion, however, most are adamant: Once a person of any age decides to have sex, nothing is going to stop him or her.

Every year more essays about sexual abuse and rape come to

"Mindworks." Some are sent anonymously, and writing the essay is the first time the child has ever told anyone what happened. Those essays frequently convey the victim's rage, pain, and confusion. But even though the kids will write about almost anything, no matter how personal or painful, one taboo seems to remain—homosexuality. Only one essay out of more than a quarter million has ever broached the topic, despite common estimates that perhaps as many as one in ten people is gay. Several years ago a teen describing himself as a "closet gay" wrote, "I'm really living a lie because I can't tell the world what's inside. It hurts so much to keep it inside, but it would probably hurt more if I told."

When teens write about sex they are capable of dispassionate analyses of sex, rhapsodies about being in love, and thoughtful essays explaining their reasons for withstanding the pressure and abstaining. They also write about such things as these: The thirteen-year-old who says people sometimes like to be tied up, the sixth-grader whose fourteen-year-old friend has two children, the several who mention that some kids perform sex for money, the seventh-grade boy who writes, "Most girls are drunk when they get laid."

In the middle of all that, one statement is particularly poignant. Nicole, 17, writes, "The right age is not supposed to be in childhood or the teen years, because that is the only time one can be a child and enjoy the precious days of youth."

■ ■ ■

I wonder about boys a lot. I wonder if they like me and what they think about me. Every night I lay in bed and think about boys. I don't know why. Maybe I'm boy crazy. I'm sure glad God invented them. — Girl, 14

■ ■ ■

I think I'm ready for sex now, but I can wait until I'm sixteen.
— **Girl, 13**

I've decided not to have sex when I'm this young because the last time I did, I made a grave mistake by having sex with the wrong girl. — Boy, 14

The right age is when their parents say so. If your parents say, "no," you'll have to wait a while. — Girl, 10

If two people cannot openly speak about sex, they are not ready to engage in it. — Boy, 18

■ ■ ■

As far as age goes, I don't believe there is one. Whether you're eighteen or thirty-five you should still wait for marriage.

— Amy, 13

It's an old-fashioned idea, but the right time to have sexual intercourse is after being married. If an engaged couple or a girlfriend and boyfriend have premarital sex, later on there will be nothing new to experience. A lot of times the relationship can become based on sex. It's like kissing—the more you kiss the more you want.

Another reason is regret. People tend to be narrow-minded. They always think that this guy is the right one. What if your fiancé asks you if you have ever had sex before? Maybe he has saved himself for you. What if your children ask you if you have had sex with any other guy than Daddy? How can a person set a good example with a guilty conscience? Waiting is a lot more romantic. — Tasha, 18

■ ■ ■

It's everyone's goal to have sex when you're married, but it's so hard because your hormones are kicking in and saying, "I want sex, I want sex!" — Chad, 17

I believe that God gave us sex to save for marriage, not to make it an adolescent toy. The best thing adults can do is set a good example for their kids. They can't say, "We don't want you to be having sex" and then go out and sleep with five other mates. — Sara, 16

The right age for sex is when you're married. But if you're a runaway and you need money, it might be okay. — Boy, 14

I hear from my parents that sex is wonderful. Teenagers might think that, too. It's different for every teenager, no two reasons are exactly the same. Some think that sex is better earlier, some think it's better later.

A good age for having sex is when you're ready and able to take care of a baby. (It's expensive.) You have to have money and time.

Adults should talk straightforwardly to kids. They should tell kids about sex, how it feels, about the rewards and consequences.

I'm going to wait to have sex. I don't want to have an unwanted baby. — Emma, 9

All teens feel they are ready to have sex. Have you ever heard a teenager ever say, "I'm not old enough to do this"? Of course you haven't. Everyone thinks they are ready. Parents cannot really stop their sons or daughters from having sex because they can't watch us twenty-four hours a day. — Boy, 15

If I just ponder the question, "Why have I already had sex?" I come up with no concrete answers. Why not? Why should I wait until I'm older? Is something this special only meant to be felt by adults? — Boy, teen

I sometimes think why wait? I'm only getting older and one more day closer to my death. — Carrie, 14

Back in the ice age people would have sex when they were physically able to just to have children, because back then, people lived to be about twenty (if they were lucky). But now, with science, we can live to be one hundred. So if you can be one hundred, why rush it? Take your time! — Girl, 12

Many kids have problems at home with their family. Sex is a way to forget their problems or use it as a form of rebellion.

Sex is used as an outlet for frustrations and to get back at or punish parents for (the child's) unhappiness.

Kids believe they will find what they lack from sex. Teens struggle constantly to gain acceptance; it is a continuous battle to keep one's self-worth and confidence. Teens see sex as a way to be accepted, as a substitute for love, self-worth, and confidence. It seems to be a fulfilling substitute for anything lacking in their lives. — Sally, 16

We also do it because it's wrong and we can get punished. There's a dangerous side to it. Teenagers like things with danger in them. It seems exciting to them. — Girl, 13

When you're going out with someone, the only thing that your friends ask is, "Did you sleep with him/her yet?" Another example is, when you're out on a date with someone your friend says, "I'll bet you don't try anything with him/her." Your reply is usually going to be, "Yeah, I'll bet you." So you make a bet with a friend and there you are, pressured into having sex.

— Boy, 15

Sex attracts men and the girls who have sex get the guys. It's sad, but true. — Boy, 17

You can't live without sex. All you do is think about sex. When you get to be thirteen years old, you get horny and you want to have sex. — Boy, 14

Most guys have sex to fulfill their male egos and most girls have sex to please their boyfriends. — Michelle, 16

If a guy is a virgin, then everyone laughs at him or thinks he's a queer. — Boy, 18

■ ■ ■

Guys do it for status. Guys keep a list of the girls they had and whoever had the most is considered the stud of all studs. Guys will tell a girl anything to get sex. — Girl, 17

Girls often get pressured into having sex by their boyfriends. Most of them have probably heard the line, "I have those needs." Maybe they should relieve those needs by lifting cars instead of harrassing their girlfriends. — Girl, 18

We went to the dance, you and I on a date. Danced and enjoyed ourselves wanting each other more as time passed. Ran out of gas on the way home. Back seat, front seat. Did it really matter?

Next day in school I'm hailed as a "stud," I'm cool, guys' envy. You're hailed much the opposite, a "slut," you're easy, girls' disgrace. You're hurt. I'm proud.

How could a view on an action be perceived so differently? How has our society become so twisted? — Chuck, 18

Guys expect to marry a virgin, but all during their high school years girls gave up their virginity to these boys. They may wonder why they should wait for bread when they can buy it and eat it all in one day. My dad once asked me, "Why should a guy have to buy a car before he test-drives it?" This just goes to show how men view women today. — Girl, 17

■ ■ ■

The generation before mine thought sex was a great way to show love. This generation thinks sex is a game. — Boy, 18

At about fifteen we feel we're old enough to make the decision. I thought I was. Come on, we know how from watching movies and most of us are rarin' to try it out, after all we do have friends who have done "IT."

At first I didn't think anyone I'd be friends with would even think about having sex until they were married. I was wrong. I discovered one of my friends had, so then I thought everyone must.

By the way she and several celebrities on TV talked, it seemed like the only thing to do.

When I was faced with becoming sexually active, my boyfriend and I talked it over and decided the risks were too high and we were too young to face the consequences. I was relieved. Several months later, I was even more relieved after we broke up. I couldn't imagine how it would have felt to see him with his friends at school if we had had sex.

Luckily, I realized that not everyone has sex and love does not revolve around sexual relations. — Girl, 16

Our society makes teens grow up faster than ever before. We begin to take care of ourselves at younger ages and we gain more responsibilities earlier in our lives. Because we grow up so fast, we assume that we are adults at younger ages than our parents did.

I don't think a person should be judged on their sexuality because often they are simply trying to grow up faster, which is what we've always been taught to do, isn't it? — Debby, 18

The problem with our society is that there is an obsessiveness with sex. It's even used to sell products. It isn't enough just to advertise a car, but there is almost always a half-dressed woman draped over it. — Nicole, 17

I figured out that adults need to have sexual intercourse at least once every month. I learned this from the love doctor on the Arsenio Hall show one night. I don't know what makes it important, but I think that they need to be loved just as much as we do. — Boy, 11

The hardest part about growing up is the pressure to have a boyfriend. We get pressure from parents, friends, romance novels, television, and movies, not to mention our own bodies. Society tells us that we have to have a boyfriend in the same way it tells us we have to shower, use toothpaste, and wear deodorant.

Girls feel they have to have boyfriends for the silliest reasons. We think we'll be considered "losers" or "loners" by our peers if we're single. Of course there's always the myths that a boyfriend will make us happy and having a boyfriend will make us feel secure.

After you get a boyfriend, there's always the pressure of sex. Society can eliminate that by putting less emphasis on having sex and concentrating more on the emotional relationship.

— Taryn, 14

The main reason teenagers experiment with sex is the plain, sensual feeling they receive from it. Everyone at some time has kissed someone, hopefully receiving a positive, loving, and arousing feeling from it. As my peers and I try to find our own self-identities, sex is almost (if not more) tempting than other matters that require a major decision, namely alcohol and drugs. Sex is directly related to a teenager's desire to experiment.

Experimenting with sex is oftentimes much more pleasing than with a chemical substance. It feels good, it's shared, it's accessible, and hopefully there are no aftereffects. I realize some may argue that the psychological and emotional damage to both partners at times can be catastrophic. I understand this, but tell me, wouldn't a parent rather deal with a talk to their child about sex (and I mean safe sex) than pick them up at the local police station high on crack? — Dax, 17

I believe that many teens are seduced by the promise of pleasure. More than one of my friends has told me that the actuality is quite different, at least at first. — Boy, 17

Everyone would like to believe that every teenaged male is out to make a conquest and every teenaged female feels she must give in. I'm sorry to burst your bubble, but this is not so.

Some teenagers may, to the amazement of nine-tenths of the adult population, actually fall in love, or at least think that they have. Not all teens just have sex for the sake of having sex. Some of us are truly in love and want to express that.

Personally, I think you should wait until you are in love to have sex. I don't think that there is an age limit to that.

So, parents, if you want to really help your children, then do just that. Make sure you leave the subject of sex open, so that your teenage son or daugher can go to you for help.

Because, no matter if you say sex is off-limits or perfectly acceptable, if a teenager is in love, your words won't change that. — Denim, 15

When kids hear the word sex, they usually laugh. But I found that as you get older, you stop the laughing and you find out how serious it really is and what it means to have sex.

— Girl, 11

I got pregnant at the beginning of this summer and I got married at the end of it. But the problem is I'm only fifteen.

I'm not saying that I regret any of it because I love my husband and my baby, but I just never expected it to happen to me. I went to a good school, lived in a good neighborhood, and had good friends. It always appeared to me that it happened to other girls, but I've learned that anything that can happen to one person can also happen to you, no matter who you are.

My advice to teenage girls is to be protected. As you can see my adult life has just started and I'm only fifteen. — Girl, 15

My life was going real great! Average grades for a new school year, a newer bigger school, great friends, a job, and last but not least, a terrific boyfriend. Then, one day, it happened. It was so scary to know that I was going to be a mom. The worst part of it was that I was only fifteen.

I knew that having this child would be the worst thing for me at my age. I had to decide between keeping it, abortion, adoption, or suicide.

When I first found out that I was pregnant, my mom was there. I remember the hurt look of disappointment in her eyes. It was too much to handle. My boyfriend was scared but determined. He had plans to keep it. He said, "I'll quit school and get a better paying job." I couldn't subject him to give up his life for the child and I. As for my dad, he wanted me to keep it. I wondered why he felt that way.

I decided on an abortion. My boyfriend was hurt and so was I. I hoped that someday he would understand my decision, even though I didn't understand it myself.

The memory of what we could've had still lingers with us but the most important part is that we are still together. We have been and always will be there for each other.

Ever since my abortion, I have felt alone, thinking about the fact that I gave up something that would've been my very own.

I have learned that, in the future I hope that I will be able to help my boyfriend and my mother when they feel alone because being lonely is a scary feeling. — Girl, 15

I will have to work a lot to support the child that I now have, and this will affect my schooling. I may not ever be able to go to college because I will have to work a lot, and if I do go to college that will mean a lot more working.

With all the working that I will be doing, I won't have much time for friends or even for the family that I am working so hard to support.

Also, my parents and siblings are disappointed with me because they felt that I had so much going for me, and because of one careless decision, I might not be able to reach my peak of success.

When I get down in the dumps from thinking about all of this, I talk to my friends or to grown-ups that I trust and I am close to. They are usually full of support and words of encouragement. After listening to them, the situation doesn't seem so hopeless, and I see that if I dedicate myself to it, I can modify my mistake. — Boy, 17

The most special thing that I have ever done was going to natural childbirth classes with my girlfriend. When Julie went into labor, I was with her the whole way. It felt so good to be part of something that I started in the first place.

Finally, when I saw the baby's head coming out, it felt so good. After they had pulled her out and laid her on Julie, the feeling was so good that there is no way to describe it.

It was so special because I got to be there. For all those fathers who have to wait to find out, they may never get the same feeling that I got being there. Throughout all of Julie's and my emotions, we stuck together. It was worth it because we have a daughter now. — Boy, 16

When people make jokes about rape this hurts my feelings the most. I was sexually abused and I know what it feels like to have other people say things about incidents that they have heard, then laugh about them. Believe me it is nothing to laugh at. Rape is the most painful experience a person would ever have to go through.

I can remember some times when people first heard what had happened to me. Some of the kids at school knew the guy. They kept telling me that I was being unfair to him. If you are ever in that situation don't listen to them, they are wrong.

My dad also hurt me when I was in this situation. When I told dad what had happened, he told me I shouldn't have been with the guy. I think this statement will stick in my mind forever and nothing I do can make me feel better about it. I just had to learn to live with it by telling myself he doesn't know what I went through. — Girl, 16

■ ■ ■

My friend met a boy that wanted to be in a gang because he thought that nobody in his family loved him. To be in the gang, he had to rape a girl and he did it. — Girl, 10

The hardest thing about growing up is worrying all your life that you're going to get AIDS. I know it sounds stupid, since I'm only thirteen, but still it's kind of scary. The worst part about it is that I'm afraid to even get married. Even now people are getting married to people they thought they knew, but really the person has AIDS. The best thing adults could do to make it easier is to teach us about it, to help to understand it better.

— Pat, 13

AIDS will become a major issue when teenagers have more friends that die from AIDS. — Girl, 16

I am not a chicken. I will never be a chicken. I don't want to be a chicken. I have been waiting to tell someone that for quite a while.

It sounds strange, I know, but my biology teacher believes that if we are not chickens now we will become one in the near future so we better learn how a chicken has sexual intercourse. You heard me right. In a unit called "Sexual Reproduction" we learned about chickens. It's as if human beings do not sexually reproduce. — Lesley, 16

The best way to teach sexual education is to be open to questions from the students. I remember my first sex education class. We were all so nervous about the whole thing. The one thing I remember, that was really helpful in getting my questions answered, is the question box. My advice to teachers teaching this subject is to be relaxed and tell your students the truth. — Girl, 16

My mom told me about the physical part of sex but we still haven't had *the talk*. *The talk* is just between my mother and me. It deals with the effects of sex and the emotional aspects. I feel that it's important that the adults can have good relationships with their teenagers. They should talk about sex in every way. — Girl, 15

I don't feel that enough parents really get across to their kids that virginity is nothing to be ashamed of. Kids never hear about how the loss of virginity can be a loss of something deep inside. — Girl, 14

My mother has been open with me, and for that I'm very thankful. She answered my questions honestly but with embarrassment. She told me that if I was planning to have sex, I should come to her and we would go get birth control. Since she was the same age as I am when she first had sex, she seems to understand. — Girl, 17

■ ■ ■

If adults are not comfortable enough to talk about sex and contraceptives with their children, they should learn. Otherwise they might have babies running around the house.

— Girl, 16

Teenagers need to know that their parents will not love them any less if they are sexually active or if they made a "mistake" at a party one night. They need to know that their parents will always love them, no matter what. When it comes to sex, teenagers need an ear to listen, not a mouth to scold. — Amy, 16

INFLUENCES

SPORTS

Sports are my life. I love hockey. I'm a goalie. I've got nine or ten shutouts and my team won first place. All the boys jumped on me, *oh my*. . . . They were heavier than twenty-eight elephants. If I could, I would watch hockey twenty-four hours a day. — Jennifer, 9

JUST LIKE AMERICANS in general, our youngsters are devoted to athletics, whether as spectators or participants. When asked if sports are important to them, kids answer with an enthusiasm that practically leaps from the page.

Quite simply, kids love sports because they make them feel good—good and sweaty, and good about themselves. "If you don't have fun when you're in a sport, then you are in it for the wrong reason," writes Derek, 13. The fun comes from the challenge, the socializing, and the escape from outside troubles.

Nicole, 13, writes, "When I'm playing on the court I don't feel like a wimpy girl. I feel like a mean, green killing machine . . ." Whatever your sentiments about her imagery, Nicole captures the deep feelings of confidence and physical mastery many kids experience while playing sports. Through sports, kids say they develop discipline, sportsmanship, cooperation, and tenacity. Many also admit to using sports to vent anger, sadness, or frustration. Younger kids say playing sports keeps them from being hyper in the classroom, making life easier for both them and their teachers.

For those who are not academically or artistically gifted, the attention received for athletic achievement is especially helpful. Travis, 16, writes, "Sports are the most important thing in my life. If it wasn't for sports, I would have dropped out of school after my sophomore year." For many, sports give kids a sense of belonging, even of family, which is especially important for those who lack such closeness at home. Sports also can provide incentive not to indulge in drugs or alcohol say lots of kids, many of whom recommend that rules against athletes drinking and using drugs be strictly enforced.

Most children wholeheartedly love pure sport, but many say that too often when adults become involved, youngsters suffer stress, hurt, and disillusionment.

"Sports aren't emphasized too much—winning is!" writes Jean, 14. Kids blame coaches for much of that attitude—coaches who play only the best players, won't work with those with weaknesses, yell at their players, and cannot accept defeat gracefully; coaches who institute severe year-round training regimens; coaches who say they'll excuse absences from practice only if someone is dying. When the fun is removed, some kids give up on sports altogether.

Many kids also criticize parents. Scott, 15, describes it this way: "You tell your boy, 'Have fun, son. Winning is not important'. . . . Practice what you preach. You bark at the ump. Yell at your son. Fight with parents from the other team. Run coaches right out of their jobs. That hardly shows your son that fun comes before winning." Donnie, 14, writes, "If a kid makes one mistake in a game and has five great plays, the first thing most parents say to them is why did you make a mistake? They don't ever say anything about the good plays."

Many kids are under too much pressure to participate, particularly from parents who were once athletes. One eleven-year-old girl writes, "I do some sports for my mom. I do some for my daddy. I do some just so I can be with my friends. I do some just for me, and those are the only ones that I really enjoy."

Angie, 14, suggests one reason for adults' overinvolvement. She writes, "It seems like parents and coaches are playing the game inside their head, trying to win an agonizing battle that they cannot physically win themselves."

Many students are annoyed by their school's emphasis on sports over other activities. For example, the morning's announcements might include the results of yesterday's football game, but not of the state music contest. A fairly common belief is that teachers give sports heroes a break in the classroom.

Kids who are not athletic report significant taunting from classmates, in and outside the gym. The degree of the split that can exist between athletes and their classmates is illustrated by the response one student received when her essay was published. Kirsten, 17, wrote an essay that was very critical of the emphasis placed on sports at her school. She wrote, "Oh, how I wish that I could be so physically fit that a great job for me would be chasing after an oblong ball and hitting and getting hit by other players so hard that it could maim me for life. I wish I could experience the thrill of being a 'jock.' But, no, I had to get stuck with a fairly decent brain." She went on to describe the difference in attention given to her and others like her when they win intellectual contests compared to that given to football players—the athletes get pep rallies and pizza parties, the academic achievers might have their victory "announced in the daily bulletin a day or two or three after it occurs."

Recently Kirsten, now in college, wrote me a letter explaining what happened when her essay was published. She was subjected to ridicule and "jeers, gestures, and painful jibes from complete strangers." She went on to say, "One day the junior varsity girls' basketball team, in its entirety, threatened me physically and verbally assaulted me with a barrage of phrases I don't care to repeat. My essay appeared in February. The harassment didn't cease until well after I graduated that spring."

Another downside to sports is injuries, which many of the kids have experienced firsthand. The fear of injury is enough to discourage some from participating. A few attribute the high injury rate to the pressure placed on kids to play like the pros. They tell of even young children checking hard in hockey or roughly sacking a quarterback as they emulate the violence they observe in professional sports.

Girls today are as passionately involved in sports as the boys, and their descriptions resonate with the same energy and love of athletic endeavor. Still, a common belief persists that fewer sports are available to them. Not only do girls want as many sports opportunities as the boys, they also want as much recognition for their athletic accomplishments.

For boys and girls, from elementary school to high school, sports is a kind of first love, and as with most loves, this one can have problems. However, most of the problems—such as the pressure to participate and to win and the inequity of opportunity and recognition—could be remedied by the adults involved in children's sports. With some changes, sports could be an exciting and beneficial love that would last our children a lifetime.

■ ■ ■

It's a hot July day. There is nothing to do. Boredom has set in on our neighborhood. This calls for a game of streetball! I get on the phone to the kids on my block.

We all meet in front of my house and I get the equipment from my garage. We get out the old, ratty, and torn bases and place them on the street. Then we get out the old ripped screen and use it as a backstop. And a board we put in the middle of the street is our pitcher's mound.

Brian walks to the pitcher's board. Kyle stations himself at first base, Jimmy between second and third, and Matt plays catcher. Chad, David, Adam, and I are the team at bat.

The game lasts four innings and takes about one hour and fifteen minutes. There are always some close plays that we argue about briefly or the dramatic home run, there are always a few of those. Sometimes we might even turn a double play! And if a car comes, we have to delay the game to let it drive through.

At the end of the game, the score is usually low and always close. But the best thing is that nobody feels bad if they lost because they had a lot of fun. — Dan, 12

If sledding was considered a sport, I might try out for the team because even if I don't have the athletic skill to stay on the sled, I enjoy tumbling into the snow. — Erica, 9

I could synchronize swim until my arms fell off and I would never be tired of it. — Amy, 11

I know a girl who loves doing homework but hates sports and she has the fattest thighs I have ever seen. — Marina, 15

Sports help me vent frustration or anger in a way less harmful than screaming or hitting somebody. — Jennifer, 13

Sports are a good way to relax your mind. After I come home from a sport my mind feels fresh and I feel awake. My home-work is easier to do and it gets done quicker after I have a chance to relax. — David, 13

Teachers like kids to be in sports because they think it will keep you out of trouble and away from parties. But I know from experience, sports doesn't prevent you from going out and getting ripped and raising hell. — Boy, 18

■ ■ ■

Sports have a magic in them. They force you to go past your abilities and learn to do things you didn't think you could do.
— Kristin, 12

I am not that smart so if I am in sports and am good at it, it will make up for my weaknesses. — Heather, 11

Right now I'm playing basketball and it helps to teach life's game: Sometimes you are on and everything works for you and when you are off nothing goes good at all. — Layton, 15

While you're running you think to yourself, "Why am I doing this? Why am I pushing myself this hard? What's the purpose of running around a park?" I answer those questions when I cross the finish line. I feel as though I accomplished something, something I've been trying to accomplish for years.

— Brenda, 14

Sports have always played a big role in my life, but only recently, when my knee injury occurred, did I realize how much they mean to me. Not being able to play basketball, and possibly not softball or volleyball, again for a couple of seasons really scares me. I am still a part of the team and support them at their games, but I feel something of major importance has been stripped from me and my life. If I cannot play for a while, I will have to find something of equal value to sports, so I can ease this empty feeling inside of me that seems to linger forever.

— Heather, 15

I am an athlete and I love sports. Yet I was denied the chance to try out for my school's wrestling team. I had had the coach's and the athletic director's approval. An official downtown without knowing who or how good/bad I am, put a stop to it. Why? Because I am a girl. That was almost enough to make me want to give up on sports. — Girl, 12

In my class when lots of boys lose a game or sport, there tends to be more complaining and excuses than when girls lose.

— Prairie, 11

When a girl is good at a sport, guys start to feel intimidated. If you mess up, they jump all over your case and tease you.

— Becky, 14

Parents make kids go out so they can have a winner. That's all that matters: Having a winner. Kids hurt from things like that. When things like that happen, sports are no longer fun. The magic is broken. — Kate, 16

Sports are very important to kids today, but society and especially parents put too much pressure on kids to perform athletically. I've helped coach hockey for younger kids and have firsthand experience with this. How can you yell at a seven-year-old to skate harder and play tough when his ankles are the only part of his skate touching the ice?

Parents spend hundreds of dollars putting their kids through the best hockey schools and even more on equipment. Then when the kids get old enough they get to try out for "traveling teams." These are (supposedly) the best players, but half the time it's politics. If your dad is an important person in the hockey program or has pull the kid may be put on the team even if he isn't the best. This is terrible to do to a kid. I've seen kids cry because they didn't make the team and then parents get upset at the kid for not making the team.

There is too much stress put on younger kids; they're not pros, they're just out for fun. Sports are important for kids, but society and parents put too much pressure on them to be superstars. Let them be kids. Just let them play. — Scott, 17

Some parents push their kids to be good at a sport, then yell at them when their grades drop. — Cathy, 11

In our family I think sports are stressed too much. Every wrestling match, football game, or baseball game I'm in, my father is always there watching. It seems to me whether I win or lose my father always criticizes me. If I do one thing wrong my family notices it. To be the best I not only think I have to beat everyone, but I must not make any mistakes. — Boy, 15

■ ■ ■

Most parents would rather say, "That's my boy, Number Fifty-one," than say "That's my boy, the nerd in the science lab." — Tricia, 14

I'm tall and big and at first my whole family wanted me to go into football but I didn't want to. But finally I gave in and played last year. I hated it. I like basketball a lot more and I wish my family would see that. — Boy, 12

Sports are important to me because I like to keep my father and grandfather happy. — Jeffrey, 16

Parents, how about next time you are about to yell, "Way to go, klutz," you yell, "Nice try, son!" As corny as it may be, it makes your son feel better. Remember, your son may not be the next Babe Ruth. Your son may be the next Howard Cosell. But love your son no matter what he is. — Scott, 15

Sports can also teach parents a lesson. They find out that a sport is only a game, but some parents never realize it.

— Joey, 11

I first started gymnastics when I was in kindergarten. Then it was just something fun to do. However, when I got older and better my coach started to single me out more. When the team would go on a break, my coach would make me work. After a while the other children started to resent me.

I soon became team captain and was supposed to tell the coach any complaints my peers had. One day the children wanted to have a meeting with me without the coach. I knew if I had the meeting my coach would be mad. If I didn't have it all my friends would be mad. The next day I resigned as captain.

I began to hate practices because my coach still made me the star. He would tell me to do a handstand on the high bar and I was completely terrified. I did it anyway because I couldn't stand up to my coach. Everyone told me how brave I was because I did the handstand, but I was really breaking inside.

Every day I would try to make myself throw up just because I was so afraid to practice. Finally I quit gymnastics and joined volleyball, basketball, and softball. I still enjoy gymnastics very much and sometimes I regret quitting. However, I don't know if I could ever go through all that again. — Gail, 13

One reason I don't play sports often is because when they pick teams I'm always the last one. I hate that because it's very embarrassing. — Suzanne, 11

I am very involved with sports but sometimes it can really hurt my feelings. Like yesterday, my very best friend wanted the glory all to herself when we were playing soccer. So she kicked me in the shin. That made me unable to finish the game.
— Marie, 11

I don't like when I get hit by a hard football. I don't like getting hit in my tummy with a hockey puck. Sports are too rough. — Laura, 8

I've studied dance since I was three years old. What I hate is when some of my friends put me down because I can't catch the ball or can't kick it high enough. I love going to gym, but when they say I'm stupid and I don't know anything, it makes me feel so angry and upset. They don't realize that I don't study sports. I'm a ballerina. I just wish they'd remember nobody's perfect. — Vanessa, 10

Sports takes its toll on grades. Last quarter my grade point average was 2.5. Last quarter was football season. This quarter I'm not playing any sports and my grade point average is 3.8.
— Ryan, 15

We shorten our school day and lose class time so that the whole school can watch a few cheerleaders do some kicks and find out who's on the football team. Yet our administration won't excuse people to go to the college fair. They say we should do that after school. — Hope, 16

When Sunday afternoon comes my dad and brothers laze around, veg out, and watch the football game. Sometimes when I'm bored, I like to sit there and watch also. However, I don't watch television—I watch my dad. It is so amusing to see him at the edge of the couch, fists clenched, face contorted, ready to bellow at the players on TV. Then he'll get all upset over some stupid play and he'll let it all out. It's absolutely ridiculous!
— Amy, 13

Sports are great to play and watch, but if you don't like sports you get put down the day after a major game on TV. You hear remarks like, "You didn't watch the game?!? What's the matter with you? Got a mental problem?" So at times like that, you learn to fake like you watched the game and agree with everyone else. — Stacy, 14

■ ■ ■

Girls have to know about sports to have a conversation with a guy. — Kristen, 11

We shouldn't pay football and baseball players so much money. We should pay them once a week, ten dollars a week.
— Jamie, 6

I like to watch sports on TV because a loose puck can't hit you when you are sitting in your living room. — Mike, 11

■ ■ ■

I never watch sports on television because it's really boring. It's like watching someone else eat ice cream. — Lucky, 13

One thing I don't like about sports is all of the fighting that goes on in hockey. The government should do something about it. — Karen, 11

■ ■ ■

If the U.S.A. won first in a national knowledge bowl, would there be T-shirts made for that? — Tonia, 13

It's clear that sports have become too important when young boys who know the averages and positions of every player in the National League are flunking history because they can't remember the dates of the Civil War. — Michelle, 18

Without sports, I wouldn't know who I was. — Heidi, 12

TELEVISION
WATCHING

Taking TV away from me would be like taking food away from any living thing. — Nick, 10

FOR MILLIONS OF American kids TV is a nearly constant companion, a staple that provides entertainment, instruction, and, some might assert, escape from reality and a productive life. Over the years thousands of kids have written about their TV viewing habits, especially when asked directly how much TV they watch and what they'd do if they couldn't watch it for two weeks.

A majority of kids who figured out their weekly TV time watch more than fourteen hours and many of them confess to watching more than twenty-eight hours weekly. They watch TV before school, after school, in the evenings, while they do homework, at friends' houses, on weekends and all day long on some holidays. One girl's weekly total came to forty-seven hours; she said her mother became "hysterical" when she found out. None of the kids include in their calculations time they spend in front of the TV playing Nintendo or watching movies on a VCR.

They enjoy watching TV because it's easy to do and provides a sort of companionship. Kids who frequently are home alone say they use TV to lessen the loneliness and cover up the disconcerting sounds of a near-empty house. Youngsters in general say they enjoy watching because the lives depicted on TV are dramatic, glamorous, and adventurous and because the stories provide relief from mundane lives and personal problems. If they watch the right programs, many say, they won't be left out of lunchroom conversations and they can belong to the crowd. Many also are quick to mention that watching no longer is a choice, they consider themselves addicted.

Two weeks without TV would prove an ordeal many say they simply couldn't survive. This pessimistic prediction prevails despite the fact that, when asked, most youngsters readily devise a litany of wonderful, creative, productive endeavors they could substitute for watching sitcoms, sleazy "news" programs and soap operas. Above all, most kids say if they didn't have TV, they'd spend their time playing. They'd play with friends, pets, and parents. They'd draw and paint, build with Legos, and swing in the park. They'd also concentrate on their homework and practice their instruments and enjoy the benefits of improvement in both. Many say they'd use the time to build connections with people and to get to know themselves better. But despite their ability to project a host of enjoyable and worthwhile activities, most still profess they'd much rather watch television.

The amount of TV watching often decreases with age. Extracurricular activities or the demands of pre-college homework or jobs preclude many older kids from slumping in front of the TV all hours of the day and night. Suzie, 14, writes, "There comes a point in our lives—somewhere past 'Sesame Street' and cartoons—where we realize there is more to life than television. School, friends, parties, and sports are definitely more fun than living life secondhand through a TV screen. If I had to go for two weeks with no TV, I think I could do it quite easily. Sure, I would miss it, but with TV, it's easy to miss out on life, too."

A few writers know about life without TV firsthand because their parents forbid it, a broken TV wasn't repaired right away, or because no TV watching was part of their punishment for some misdeed. Most found the experience difficult initially, but many admit that eventually they discovered that life without the tube is possible and can even be satisfying. One ten-year-old boy, however, whose family has five TVs in the house, was grounded without TV privileges for two weeks. Because he couldn't bear being denied TV, he borrowed a mini-TV from his friend, hid in his closet, and watched for hours until he was caught.

Living without a television for several days led one teenager to an observation that might be useful for all kids (and adults) to keep in mind when considering the issue of TV watching. John writes, "When you're watching TV do you ever notice that people on TV are hardly ever watching TV? Maybe without TV our lives could be as exciting as theirs."

■ ■ ■

I love television! If somebody never invented it, think how bored everyone would be. Now that we have TV practically no one is bored.

If I couldn't watch TV, it would be like an alcoholic who couldn't have a drink. I watch it when I wake up, before I leave for school, when I get home, and before I go to bed, plus all the times in between.

So you see, I love TV! If TV wasn't invented, I'd probably invent it myself! — Sommer, 11

Some say television is like an addictive drug and I agree with them. After all, what can you say about a kid who knows more about Vanna White than Eleanor Roosevelt? — Meghan, 15

I watch seven hours of TV a day. On Saturdays I watch eighteen hours. I am really addicted.

When I'm bored, I go to the fridge and get a pop. Then I make popcorn and plunk down and watch TV. I watch more TV than my mom and dad put together. I watched thirteen hours of TV a day over Christmas vacation last year.

I get in trouble for watching TV. I never get my chores done and my mom yells at me to get them done. I try to break the habit, but I just can't do it. My parents hardly watch TV at all and I watch way too much. Some days I can't watch TV so I watch movies on the VCR.

When I grow up, my children will not be allowed to watch as much TV as I do now. I hope they will read more than watch TV. If I try, I can break the habit, but it is going to be hard. My mom and dad will help me, I'm sure.

I hope other people never watch as much TV as I do.

— Eric, 10

I usually watch thirty hours of TV a week. My mom's boyfriend says TV is my idol. — Girl, 9

Our family watches TV together from 7 P.M. to 10:30 P.M. On Sundays we watch TV from noon to 10:30 P.M. I assure you, without TV, life would be different! — Boy, 14

I think my mom and dad would have fewer headaches if I didn't watch television because my sister and I always fight over what channel we want! — Hallie, 10

■ ■ ■

When our TV set was broke down, it was gone for about two weeks. My mom kept saying that she wasn't going to get it fixed. I knew she was kidding, of course, because she would probably die without it. — John, 17

If you have homework and your mom and dad are watching TV, and you need help on it really bad, your parents don't want to be interrupted. That's when I hate TV the most.

— Girl, 10

If someone asks me a question, I tend to give a short, quick answer. That usually ends the conversation and I hate myself for it later. I usually leave the burden of conversation totally to other people. I think part of this may come from watching too much TV. Sometimes I find myself just watching a conversation instead of taking part in it. — Casey, 15

When I watch TV I feel lazy, like I haven't done anything. Being lazy puts me in a bad mood.

Lots of people are constantly watching TV and normally when they just sit there, they don't feel good about themselves. Feeling good about yourself is very important.

I think everybody should have a break from TV.

— Shelly, 11

I often abuse television, watching whatever is on when I'm bored or using it to break an unbearable silence—to deal with a TV show rather than my life and my problems. These occasions constitute more than half of my viewing time.

— Boy, 17

■ ■ ■

Watching TV is a bad idea because it wrecks your brain. My brain is already wrecked and now it is hard for me to think.

— Erica, 10

Living without TV for two weeks would haunt me for the rest of my life. — Danielle, 9

■ ■ ■

No TV would be like no pets. You love your pets just like TV. — Boy, 10

Without TV I'd go crazy and die of lack of TV watching. The good point would be after I die, I'd never mind missing another TV program again. — Joe, 9

For me, no TV would be awful. I love to put myself in the characters' places, work out their problems, etc. TV is one outlet where I don't have to be a super student, model child, and great older sister. — Roberta, 14

What would I do instead of watching TV? I would go get a job to earn some money to buy a TV. — Shane, 10

I watch one or two hours of TV every day. If I had to live without TV for two weeks, I would play. I would ride my bike. I would build lots of things like a go-cart. I would go to the dump and look for wheels.

Maybe I would build a boat out of wood. Then I would paint it red and black. In the mornings before school, I would play Legos with my sister. It would be good to have no TV because I could play more, and I would read and figure out good things to do. It would be bad to have no TV because then I couldn't see exciting things happen on TV. Sometimes I just rest in front of the TV.

One other bad thing: My bird, Robin, likes the sound of TV. He would miss the sound. — Andy, 6

I haven't watched TV for 202 days. I don't plan to watch TV for another 163 days, with the following exceptions: planned parties, school assignments, parent-approved videotapes.

The reason I plan on not watching TV for one year is because my dad and I agreed that if I don't watch TV for one full year, he will buy me a new ten-speed bike (under two hundred dollars), without my having to pay a single penny.

When I first started not watching TV, I couldn't find anything to do. Then it became a habit and I found other things to do. I read and did more with my friends and family.

The good things about not watching TV were that I got extra credit for reading more books and my grades got higher because I had more time to do my homework. The bad things about not watching TV were that I wasted my time at first because I couldn't find anything to do.

Otherwise, not watching TV has been very good for me.

— Christina, 11

If my TV was gone for about, let's say, two weeks, I'd mourn for about a minute, and then go to the library. — Carlin, 12

I like not having a TV because I like other things. I like to sew. I like to play. And I like to talk with my mom and dad.

— Laura, 6

Since I live on a farm, I don't have any kids for neighbors, so instead of watching TV for two weeks, I would play with my cats. At least cats are real, not on a screen, and I can really touch them. — Danylle, 11

■ ■ ■

If I didn't watch TV for two weeks my assignments would get done and my grades would skyrocket. — Karla, 12

As I walk past the TVs in the department store, what I see fulfills my quota of TV watching for the week. I was raised in a family where TV is against religious beliefs, which explains why I see so little of it.

When I hear discussions about the horrors of life without a TV for two weeks, I wonder, "Why?" I could never fit the idle hours of watching TV into my busy life. I wonder what I might not have accomplished in exchange for time spent sitting in front of a TV.

I deliver ninety papers before school each morning. I also have a job in a toy store and work as many as thirty hours a week. The money I earn allows me to travel a lot. I spent a month in Europe this summer. Good grades also are important to me so I must study to keep them up. I sew, play soccer, and have put in over two hundred volunteer hours at a hospital. I also enjoy reading. I could never stay up watching the late shows—I'd be too tired to perform in school and at work.

TV is a wonderful invention that has been much abused. If in any way a TV would have taken away from my sensitivity, creativity, healthy lifestyle, or closeness with my family, then I'm fortunate I never had one. — Cammy, 17

When you can't watch TV you are forced to think. You can't have creativity without thinking. When creativity goes up, boredom goes down. If you can be creative, you don't really need TV. — Jay, 12

Going without a TV set couldn't be that bad. Just think of all the people who lived before television was invented. They didn't die because they couldn't watch a soap opera.

— Laurie, 15

I don't watch much TV so I don't think it would make a difference if I couldn't watch TV for two weeks. Now if you took away my stereo, that's another story altogether. I'd end up in the loony bin making rag rugs with blunt scissors.

— Katie, 14

VIOLENCE ON TV
AND IN MOVIES

It's cool seeing people being blown up, shot, squished, and chopped. — Boy, 8

THINK BACK. When did you see your first memorable scene of movie or TV violence? Was it the chariot races in *Ben Hur?* Marshall Dillon in a shootout? The shower scene from *Psycho?* King Kong swatting airplanes from atop the Empire State Building? Whenever and whatever it was, you can bet it was very mild compared with what most children today are viewing, sometimes daily.

When we asked children how they feel about watching violent TV shows and movies, some praised the gore while others deplored the polluting of children's minds. But the most overwhelming impression is that a very common attitude among today's youngsters is, "I love violence. Violence is cool."

The essays reel with descriptions of mayhem, mutilation, and unlimited cruelty. The kids describe with delight bludgeonings, brains splattering, and blood streaming everywhere. They relate scenes of throats being ripped open and faces being obliterated. They offer visions of people being slashed, pummeled, shot, crushed, and annihilated by every means possible. In their writing they mention the movie scenes that have remained with them— heads exploding, people being skinned alive, scenes of entrails from dismembered villains, with a heart still beating in the middle of it all. They describe the evil characters they've watched stalking innocent ones, often teenagers and women, and hatcheting them to death. They love the scenes where everybody and everything blows up. For most of these kids, movie mass slayers Freddie Krueger and Jason are as familiar as Santa Claus and the Easter Bunny.

But despite all this attraction to violence, many do maintain standards for how much they can take. Some draw the line at gross scenes of dismemberment that make them want to puke; a couple say it is not okay to kill children or animals; a few propose that all scenes of sexual violence should be banned. Others declare they need and want and even crave more violence, and the more gruesome the better.

They enjoy violence, most say, because violence means action, suspense, thrills, excitement, and escape from their "boring" lives. The kids like the power they feel when a bad guy gets his and the adrenaline rush when the "good" guy's in danger. A couple, however, say they really like it when the good guy gets killed and wish that would happen more often. Many like the feeling, or purport to like the feeling, of being terrified.

One common rationale for approving of the amount of violence is that it only reflects the reality of America today. Hence, the violence is actually educational, they say—it prepares young people for the real world. Some even believe violent shows are instructional because they give hints on how to shoot when a stranger hassles you or what a woman should do when she's assaulted.

For others, however, the violence appeals because it's not like real life. They enjoy the fake blood, the special effects, and the novelty of seeing things they might never see in real life, like a face melting or someone chainsawing off somebody else's arm. Among this group are those who also believe much of the most gruesome and overdone violence is amusing and campy.

Hundreds link TV and movie violence to the increase in violent crime in society, but most say the movies don't influence them to copy the characters' behavior. Only wackos and psychos who should have been locked up years ago are inspired to do that, they say. But many admit to having disturbing thoughts and observing more aggressive behavior in themselves and their peers during and after they watch violence. Many babysitters comment on the changes they see in their charges when they've watched violent programs. They see young kids attacking family members and friends with karate kicks, hurling kitchen knives into the wall, pretending to punch, shoot, and strangle whomever happens to be within range. Many are particularly tired of the miniature Teenage Mutant Ninja Turtles wreaking havoc in households and in city parks. According to one student, her school created a rule against Ninja Turtle play-acting on the playground because too many kids were getting hurt.

About half of those who wrote say they might want some of the violence lessened, but the majority say that at least some must remain because without violence, stories are boring. Anna, 16, writes, "To not have violence on TV would be like not having a front door on your house: Something would be missing." Many, however, are disgusted when too many people die too quickly and messily and want the moviemakers to hold it down to two, or maybe five, killings per show, with slightly less blood and guts. Dozens say keep the mayhem, but, please, no swearing. The swearing is far more offensive to them than the violence. Others want to see violence used only when it reflects something real, like war, for instance, or a true story. For many, violence is acceptable if the story has a moral, the good guys win, and the villains are punished.

What is particularly dismaying about reading the younger children's reactions is that so many use these words to describe how violence makes them feel: scared, sad, and mad. Many say the violence makes them cry. They hide under pillows, duck under blankets, or huddle against parents' shoulders while they watch. Hundreds of all ages describe vivid nightmares from too large doses of violence. They go to bed terrified, sometimes crawling in with mom and dad to ward off the images that haunt them in the dark. Teens recall their own nightmares and daymares brought about when they viewed too much violence too young.

The impression is that violence causes a lot of discomfort and anxiety in kids, but, unfortunately, the children often don't seem to tell anyone how frightened they are. Judging from these and other essays, one reason may be because the children suspect their parents enjoy watching violent shows. Because they want to share whatever time they can with their parents, they'll watch whatever their parents are watching. They also fear they'll be considered wimps by siblings and peers if they admit to their fear. In addition, many kids seem to consider themselves powerless to walk away. Fourth-grader Anne writes, "When I watch violent movies I feel scared, shy, and afraid to move. I think someone should invent a channel changer so if you press a button if violence comes on it will automatically turn it off!"

Although many young children write of how frightening they find violent shows, others proclaim their love of violence. One seven-year-old girl writes, "When I watch a TV show that has violence in it I feel like I want to go upstairs to watch it in color." Little boys write with great machismo of how they love the violence; they describe with relish their favorite killing scenes.

This love of violent programs extends to both girls and boys of all ages. One impression, however, is that boys enjoy all of the types of violence, especially those concerned with warfare and violence that is very graphic. Girls seem to prefer violent movies with suspenseful plots and slightly less gore.

For some their responses to TV violence is affected by the amount of personal violence in their lives—the violence that occurs when Dad gets drunk, for instance. One eleven-year-old writes, "I like watching violent movies and TV shows because my family argues a lot. I can pretend I'm Jason and I'm killing my family." A twelve-year-old boy writes, "When I was about nine or ten I always got kicked around by my dad. I grew up with violence. If I am watching *Lethal Weapon 2* and somewhere in Colombia a drug lord's servants try to kill this guy because he's a cop, it's fine with me if he shoots back." On the other hand, young people who have had a classmate raped and strangled or a brother severely beaten by a gang of toughs or a father shot to death, say they've lost their appetite for violence on the tube or movie screen.

Those most opposed to the violence worry that their peers who are addicted to it are becoming numb, that death doesn't seem to matter, that their values are being skewed. They don't like the queasiness they feel when they watch people being tortured and they don't like having to muster their courage to watch these shows at slumber parties where everyone else seems to think it's all so wonderful.

Many of the older kids recognize that part of why they enjoy the violence and are not disturbed by it is because they've been exposed to it from their earliest years. One boy, whose mother took him to *Robocop,* an R-rated movie considered among the most violent of the season's movie offerings, when he was seven, says that then he was terrified by the violence; now he enjoys it. Some say they barely notice the killing anymore unless it's more extreme than what they've seen before. Another common perception is that watching violence truly is addictive, that the more you see, the more you need, the more you watch.

Reaction to cartoon violence is mixed. Some suggest that seeing Wile E. Coyote plummeting off a cliff or being smashed by an anvil for the millionth time is as damaging as watching Arnold Schwarzenegger machine-gunning the multitudes. Others disagreed: All kids know cartoons are fake, they say, so no negative effects are likely.

An amazing number express concern that younger kids can't handle the violence and set some limits on when kids should be allowed to see it. Even children seven or eight or nine years old worry about children younger than they are seeing too much violence. Twelve is a common age after which unlimited violence is considered okay, but some place the limit far younger, for instance, age four.

Many suggest that TV should be toned down or kept the same to protect younger children. Others propose that TV violence be shown only after children are in bed or only on a cable channel devoted to violent shows. Most consider the movie ratings system a farce because it's rarely enforced at theaters and almost never at video stores. Others make the point that PG-13 and even PG movies are increasingly violent so the ratings system simply doesn't protect the youngest kids.

Scores who are concerned about the amount of violence blame parents who don't monitor what their kids watch, who don't continually explain to children what is real and what isn't, who insist on satisfying their own thirst for violent entertainment regardless of its effects on the children around them. Several of the young people write that they will never allow their children to see as much violence as they've seen.

As to why people create these shows, there is nearly universal agreement—megabucks. Many also say these programs are created because adults love violence, too; that there is something within the human psyche that is and always has been fascinated with cruelty and gore.

The debate as to whether viewing violence has a long-term or negative effect on children probably will continue for years, but one thing is very clear from these children's essays. Many if not most of our children have been exposed to large quantities of brutal, ugly, and evil images on television and in movies. Their descriptions of the violence they have viewed and its effects upon them paint a picture of children whose innocence has been poisoned and eroded. That innocence can never be restored.

Rebecca, 15, writes, "When my family is watching TV and my sister runs out of the room scared, I know something's wrong with television today. You may be thinking, 'She's a kid! What can you expect?' I think we can expect a lot. The instinct inside my sister and all children tells them what is frightening, what is not good for them. You used to have that instinct before you became accustomed to violence. Do you remember?"

■   ■   ■

I don't mind violence on TV and movies at all. I just don't like all the disgusting stuff (brains, heads rolling, blood, guts, etc.). But violence doesn't bother me. Violence *should* be in movies and on TV. It makes them more suspenseful and exciting.

Violence is an important part of TV and movies. People have to learn that life isn't a garden and the Teenage Mutant Ninja Turtles are perfectly good role models for kids. The Ninja Turtles are antidrugs and anticrime, and that's good enough for me (*Cowabunga, dudes!*). — Emily, 12

When I watch TV, I look for violence. No violence, I change the channel. Some shows have heavy violence like people getting mutilated or skinned alive and some have light violence, like stabbing or drive-by shootings. — Shaun, 12

■ ■ ■

If we don't have scary movies and TV shows, the world will be no fun. — Alisha, 10

I like violence, but not when it is real. I like it because it makes my heart pound faster and faster and it makes my eyes focus harder. And best of all, when my parents tell me to do something I can't hear them because I am focusing so hard on the TV. — Jason, 11

When I watch movies that contain violence I feel excited and grossed out at the same time. — Mel, 11

I like some violence, but when there is so much that you think you are going to throw up, it ruins the show.

— Sam, 12

If there was no violence in James Bond movies, all there would be is kissing, and nobody wants to watch that unless they're on a date. — Scott, 10

I like violence because of the blood. I like when they get stabbed. I would want more violence because I like violence.

— Jill, 8

Ripping people up with knives and axes isn't my type of movie. I do like movies with grenades and guns, like war movies. It's different because they don't show you ten minutes of killing someone when they're already dead. — Kevin, 11

They include violence to make the movies more exciting and because big men have to be strong like warriors. Some people expect men to be strong and violent. — Ben, 11

■ ■ ■

Everyone should have a little violence in their life. This would be a very boring planet if everybody went around giving flowers to one another. — Mark, 12

Somehow all this violence attracts us. It's just like the television and movie writers have a magnet pulling you towards the violence. — Ann, 12

Violence in movies and TV has a definite effect on me. I generally don't consider myself a violent person, but after watching a violent movie, I'm exhilarated. — Girl, 17

I feel excited when I hear there is a violent movie on TV. I'm scared when I see the bad dudes that are all mangled up and bloody. I'm sorry after someone nice is killed. I'm glad after they catch the bad dudes and kill them and bury them. I would like to see more violent movies on TV because I like big weapons and the blood gushing out of people, like water coming out of a faucet. — Jeff, 12

Sometimes violence is nice. If you want to hit someone or hurt someone you can sit down in front of TV and watch someone do it for you. — John, 12

Violence is sometimes a mood I have. Sometimes I feel as if it's me against the world and watching things blow up makes me feel better. — Dana, 13

People like to watch violence because it makes them feel strong. It's easier to be angry than it is to be kind. It takes longer to be kind. — David, 9

The violence on TV and films doesn't bug me. When you have been around and near TV for fifteen years, you grow immune to the violence. But the idea of violence does bug me. Ask yourself, what kind of a world do we live in when we don't have enough polio and measles vaccines, but we have a violence vaccination. Why? — Jason, 15

Violence is great. It prepares us for what might happen for real. It tells us how strong we are and if we can handle gore. I mean, how many times a day do you see someone getting their head blown off? If it wasn't for violence in TV and movies, we might never know how it looks! We need more violence because it expands our imagination and people who are always good get to see a different side of things. — Reed, 14

You have to have some exposure to violence or a person would be naive. If you are naive, you will become a victim.
— Adam, 11

I watched a news special on our invasion of Panama. What I saw will probably always haunt the back of my mind. They showed Panamanian citizens lying face down in their own pools of blood, mutilated bodies being dragged to huge, mass graves that were being bulldozed over. The worst part was that weeks later the people of Panama were missing relatives and were not informed so the mass graves were opened and bodies were dragged out partly decomposed.

These macabre scenes were all displayed on our good ol' nightly news. This to me is far worse than Freddie Krueger or a few actors acting out a murder. This left an impression I'll never forget unlike any TV show or movie. It's easy to grab the remote and click the tube off and forget about an episode of ''Twin Peaks,'' but it's a little hard to avoid reality.

— Julie, 17

■ ■ ■

As a kid, life is pretty scary. We don't need violence to scare us more than we already are. — Lori, 10

I feel scared when I'm watching a scary movie at night because when it's over, I have to go to bed. Then my nightmares begin. — Brady, 10

Some scary movies make me feel sad because some people I like in the movie die. Other movies make me feel mean and I don't like to feel like that. There are other movies that make me feel tough and I like to feel like that. — Jacob, 10

■ ■ ■

I want to see less violence because it makes me soooo scared. I feel like I am going to get killed. — Rita, 7

I would like movies to be less violent because I think they promote the use of violence. My brother gets so scared sometimes he won't sleep in his room because he thinks someone is going to come and shoot him through his window while he is sleeping. — Karie, 15

My stomach turns when a character we know from the story dies. I am afraid that if people don't feel this emotion when people die on television, then maybe they could easily kill somebody in real life. It is a scary thought. — Dave, 14

Producers should put less violence on TV because it sometimes makes little kids get bad dreams during the night and then the parents have to get up and they might get tired at work and that's not good. — Erin, 8

If I have to watch these movies at my friend's house, I close my eyes at the gory parts and try to think about ice cream, cake, or something I like. — Lisa, 13

I've noticed that after I watch a violent show or movie I'm usually in a bad mood or depressed. My mom says that they pollute the brain. I believe her because of what I've seen in myself after a violent movie or show. — Sasha, 14

I would like to see less violence on TV because it puts bad thoughts in your mind that you can't erase. — Jason, 11

Violence is not a very good thing in movies and TV shows. For one, it gets my brothers all wound up. They run around the house chasing each other with toy guns, knives, and swords. Then that night they have bad dreams and scream and wake up the whole house. Also, when I watch violence all it does is run through my head for two weeks. — Logan, 11

My mom's friend has a little boy who watched "Teenage Mutant Ninja Turtles" and tried to act like them. He hit his sister over the head with a wooden puzzle. His mom wouldn't let him watch it anymore. After a while, she decided he could watch it once a week. After the first time watching it, he hit his little sister in the stomach with a bat. — Shannon, 12

I don't think violence should be taken completely off the air, but when I hear the kids I babysit saying they want to grow up to be fighters and shoot people, I know something's wrong.
— Michelle, 12

My friend's dad is really into violent movies and shows. He *really* likes fighting, shoot-outs, and blood and guts. His four-year-old son watches this stuff with him and this kid is a terror. He runs around the house kicking, biting, pinching, hitting, and screaming all because this is what he watches on TV all the time. — Shannon, 11

Sometimes I feel very violent and it doesn't feel very good. I keep saying to myself, "Dani, stop thinking that way." On the other hand, sometimes I feel anxious and excited. I like it when the bad people get killed. Sometimes I feel like going in the movie and hurting the person badly and it feels bad.

— Dani, 10

I think most boys would be nicer if they did *not* watch TV violence. — Elizabeth, 10

I don't agree with people that say watching violent movies will cause people to do crazy things. I feel if their parents teach them right from wrong, it should be no problem. — Adam, 16

Television violence has no effect on inner feelings or the way people act. If it did, wouldn't people turn into clowns by watching cartoons? — Paul, 16

There are a lot of unnecessarily violent shows on TV. Shows that portray rape as the main plot are harmful to people who have lived through a rape.

Shows have a rape or an attack and then some bigshot cop or private investigator comes in, gets the guy, puts him in jail, and makes everything perfectly all right for the victim. This is a totally naive way to look at it because in real life it often takes months and sometimes years for cops to solve a case and no one makes it all right.

The public is getting the wrong impression from these violent shows that everything is taken care of and that there is not a problem. There *is* a problem. I've lived through it more than once and no one comes flying in to save the day and *no one* can make everything all right, especially not in the two hours it takes to run these shows. — Girl, 14

There should be absolutely no sexual violence on the air because it gives everybody bad ideas. — Angie, 11

■ ■ ■

I do not like violence because my mom and dad are violent. I feel real mad about it. — Girl, 9

I hate violence because I think it makes the people at home want to hurt someone. So they take it out on their kids.

— Girl, 9

I don't like the parts when men kill or hurt the women. It's real mean of men to do that. — Christa, 9

Violence is bad because it hurts many people. It teaches us to hit and be mean to women and others. Violence is not just a physical but also a mental hurt. If you get yelled at a lot, it makes a person mad inside. He keeps it inside until it hurts so bad he cries and thinks about it for a long time. Violence makes no sense. It is gross and mean. — Kurt, 11

You really don't understand just what death is like until someone close to you dies. Just last night a friend got crashed by a car. It's not fair, and no way should death and violence be good entertainment. — Barrett, 15

■ ■ ■

Violence on television is turning the world into a junkyard.
— Marie, 9

It's obvious why so many movies and TV shows have violence as a main theme: It sells. That's not rocket science. For some reason people enjoy bloodshed and gore. It's part of the human mystique—we enjoy watching what we ourselves would never

even think of doing. Porno movies sell for the same reason.
— Tom, 17

People who write and produce movies and TV shows with a lot of violence must like those kinds of shows and feel that people like them, too! I don't think they know how many young kids watch them and get horrified and feel unsafe every minute of their lives. — Molly, 12

I'm sure that when the TV producers themselves were children, they were scared of violent shows, so it isn't very smart of them to produce stuff like that. — Samantha, 8

People write TV shows with violence because people are mad at each other. — Patti, 8

It's not right for little kids like us to watch shows that are rated R, but some kids' parents don't seem to care. I think parents should care more about their kids. I think people make violent TV movies and TV shows because lonely people like that stuff and they have nothing else to do. — Erin, 11

I'm sure parents would rather explain violence than sex.
— Sloane, 13

For as long as I can remember, everything I watch or listen to has been carefully censored by my parents. I thank them for this because the people who should be doing this, the people who rate the movies and produce the shows, seem unaware of what's happening to Americans. We try too hard to appear too tough. It seems as if in the movies, you're only a hero if you can beat up the bad guy. — Liz, 12

My mom told me that when she was growing up and watching television she thought that everyone's problems would magically work themselves out. On the shows she used to watch, everything would always turn out in the end, so she believed her life would be that way, too. Is the new generation of children going to feel that the world is full of violence and think that their lives will be also? — Heather, 16

Why can't they have old black and white movies where someone was tied to the train track and his/her hero saves them? Nowadays they won't save them, they'll just let them get run over by the train. — Jene, 10

If we want the violence to stop, it's not the entertainment industry we must change, it's ourselves. — Bob, 14

When I look back on my childhood, I consider myself lucky. My mom and I were very close and she taught me some important things, among them to be kind, fair, and diplomatic— or at least to try to be these things. I cringe inwardly when I see violence on TV or in a movie because it goes against everything my mother ever taught me.

It frightens me when I think of what our generation is being exposed to. Violence seen repeatedly is like a hammer, assaulting protective walls of innocence and sensitivity. Seeing things over and over softens the impact, making things that should be unthinkable, like murder and rape, common, almost expected occurrences.

Children learn values from what they are exposed to most. I was lucky; I got mine from someone who cared about me. But now, in many cases, it's television that children are exposed to most. What is society teaching its children? Whose set of values is our generation learning? — Crystal, 15

■ ■ ■

When I become a father, I might let my kids watch violence, but not as much as I did. — Adam, 12

DRUGS

Kids don't take drugs to be cool. That faded out a few years ago. Now kids are thinking drugs help them deal with life.
— **Paula, 18**

ATHLETES DIE OF cocaine overdoses while crack babies languish in intensive care units. Colorful beer ads enliven sports broadcasts, drug dealers prowl the streets, and alcoholism poisons many American homes. In a society of pervasive drug use live impressionable young people—some who "just say no" and others who don't.

When asked why kids use drugs, many base their answers on personal experience. "If, just for a little while, you could be worry-free and forget all your problems and troubles just by popping a few pills, shooting up with a needle, or sniffing a little something, wouldn't you?" writes a fifteen-year-old girl. Many kids say drugs are used to ease the pain of feeling unloved by their parents, to relieve depression or boredom, to cope with rejection, loss, and loneliness.

A young person's drug use they say can be a cry for help or attention from alcoholic, workaholic, or abusive parents. Drugs also provide an outlet for kids who feel they can't live up to parental expectations. One teen writes, "Our town is filled with the kind of kids who have too much pressure put on them. The people live in a higher class and the parents expect the kids to do no wrong.

. . . Kids need to relieve the pressure, so they turn to drugs." Drug use, some say, is a way for kids who have given up to commit slow suicide.

Some kids use drugs because their idols—rock musicians, movie stars, athletes, or the most popular kid in class—use them.

For many, as fifteen-year-old Jennifer explains, peer pressure is to blame: "Nobody likes being an outcast or the chicken of the party. The only way they think they can be cool is to be like everyone else and take the drug. Little do they know that one small word can help them: No! But 'no' doesn't work all the time. When the odds are twenty-four to one, it becomes pretty scary. You forget about your parents' warnings, you forget about the commercials on TV, and you forget about your own beliefs. All you can think about is the drug. You know it can hurt you, but that doesn't matter anymore. What matters now is being one of them."

Drugs help some kids to relax, lose weight, or to ease the tension before tests and athletic games. A seventeen-year-old boy writes, "I haven't ever taken drugs before in my life except for this football season. I took speed before every game. I didn't do it to be cool or anything. I did it because speed makes me more intense and I think more clearly on just the game. I didn't do it because I like it or it made me feel good, because after the games, and the mornings after, I regretted it severely."

Using drugs can be an act of defiance or an adventure. It also can be a means for high-achieving kids to shed their "goody-goody" image and for kids who are angry with their parents to take revenge.

Some say they simply like the way drugs make them feel. "Nobody I have ever come across uses drugs for any other reason than they like it," writes a fourteen-year-old user who is trying to stop. Other users concur, saying the drugs heighten a user's imagination and deepen his or her character. A fourteen-year-old girl writes that kids use drugs because they enjoy the "good feeling of flying. You feel as if you don't have to worry about anything because it's like you're in your own world, that nobody can stop you from doing anything."

Some kids use drugs because their parents do, including a girl,

14, who writes from a treatment center, "About two years ago my father let me drink with him and that was when I started using drugs." It's easy for kids to use drugs, say most, because they're cheap and readily available. A few believe the very emphasis on not taking drugs encourages their use. Matt, 14, writes, "Kids take drugs because of everyone telling them how scary it is. It arouses everyone's curiosity enough that they wonder, 'Could it be that weird?' "

Young people would fight drug use with solutions ranging from legalizing drugs to executing dealers, instituting random drug searches at school to offering scholarships to kids who stay or get straight. Many say anti-drug programs focusing on real-life stories of users and including sessions on self-esteem can be effective. Such education, they say, cannot begin too early. Some recommend it begin in kindergarten.

For many, the best deterrent comes from the worst experience: observing the devastation caused by a loved one's drug use. One young teen describes how she watched a friend lie comatose on a respirator because of a drug overdose. An eleven-year-old writes that her eighteen-year-old cousin had been shot to death during a drug deal, and another girl saw her friend suffer from drug withdrawal at age seventeen, after having been an alcoholic for six years. But one twelve-year-old, who has seen his sisters go in and out of treatment and his brother-in-law go to jail for drug-related crimes, writes: "I've been on drugs since fourth grade. . . . I already ruined my life."

Adults are the primary cure, say those who wish adults would do more to stop the drug trafficking. Emily, 9, wants a president who "tries as hard as he can to stop drugs, so when I have kids the drug problem has stopped and I won't have to worry about my kids."

The most important first step, according to many, is that parents must realize that drug abuse can and does happen everywhere to all kinds of kids. A thirteen-year-old from a medium-sized town writes, "My parents thought we'd get away from all the drugs and stuff moving from the Twin Cities, but if they knew all the people I know that take drugs, they would probably die." A sixteen-year-old writes, "It's not just the bad kids taking drugs because I go to parties at kids' house who are athletes, honor students, etc. I can't remember a party where there wasn't alcohol and/or other drugs."

Parents and other adults also need to intervene when necessary. A junior high school student writes, "So many of the teachers at our school are thoroughly aware that there are several avid drug users in our school, but they have done absolutely nothing to help the kids cure their problem. It seems as if they are afraid to help for fear of getting in too deep."

A few acknowledge that regardless of any prevention programs, some kids will try drugs no matter what.

The issue of kids and drug use is a complicated one involving societal attitudes, government policy, and the quality of children's lives at home. Despite that, perhaps the easiest and best prevention to a child's drug use is expressed by Toby, 14. He writes, "Let your kids know you love them and they are special. Don't make them want drugs for love."

■ ■ ■

Kids use drugs because they are part of our society. We take aspirin when we have a headache, or take pills to relieve all the pains we have. So, why not take drugs when we are feeling down or bored? — Jason, 15

■ ■ ■

A lot of people take drugs because they are afraid to face reality. When you're high, nothing hurts you and nothing seems to matter. — Girl, 15

A big reason why many teens take drugs is because of the lack of attention that many of their parents give. What I mean is that when the parents divorce or become so involved with their work they lose track of their kids, then money becomes the attention that they give. It fills the void for a short time, but after a little while the kids want the attention that counts from their parents. Kids start to figure that they can get this attention by going against what parents say is wrong. After a while, drugs become a part of the way they go about this. The friends I have who have used, all fall under this category.

— Mike, 15

Teenagers have a lot of problems to cope with. They may have no friends or family they can turn to, so they turn to drugs. Drugs help them forget how crummy life is and even may have them thinking they are handling their problems well. Drugs may be the only friend that person has. — Gail, 15

I think that how people get addicted is that maybe your grandpa died and you feel like you're going to cry, but then you think that your friends will laugh so then you hold it in, but after you hold it in for a while, you start to feel sick and if someone asks you to take drugs, you say, "yes" and it makes you feel so good that you need more and more until your life depends on it and then you can't stop. — Brandl, 9

I don't think many kids are taking drugs to be cool anymore. That was an excuse used in the 70s. The main reason is extreme depression. There are so many things for a kid to worry about these days, like AIDS, the environment, and World War III. Sometimes, I wonder if I'll live to old age. — Gina, 14

Drugs are considered cool by teenagers because they are being rebellious. It was the same type of thing in the 1960s, when the hippies had communes, flower power, and protests.

— Ann-Marie, 14

It seems to me, that there is such a crusade against drugs that the more kids hear they shouldn't take drugs, the more they like doing it. It's like a game, a big challenge.

— Traci, 17

One reason drugs are considered cool is because it is a quick way to belong to something. The druggie group will accept anyone as long as they use. — Cathy, 14

The kid has languished at the party for two hours already, and he will go on doing it at least that long before he can get a ride home. Too shy to step into the merry-go-round of activities, he sits in a corner, away from the party.

Suddenly an obscure friend hands him a vial, saying, "Man, you can't miss a party like this!" The poor kid looks at the powder, then gets up and walks into the bathroom. Minutes later, he vaults out, and into the center of the group. He dances, teases, fights, and sings like a fiend for the rest of the night. No one can deny him, he is the King! And you ask why drugs are considered cool? When first used, they cure the most feared social ill, shyness. — David, 16

Now most of my friends drink and think it's really cool. Well, I think drinking is a drag. I have gallons of peer pressure coming at me every time I go out. — Tim, 14

If I were ever to take drugs, it would be for curiosity. I honestly wonder if it is as great as people say. It must be something exciting because drugs are very popular.

I know there is that saying that if your friends want you to do drugs they are not your friends, but be real. You don't think about that because losing all your friends is the scariest thing to happen to a kid. — Heather, 16

The possibilities of a kid not seeing a commercial advertising liquor is very unlikely. There is one at almost every commercial break. Liquor commercials are also one of the biggest supporters of sporting events. Have you ever seen a football or baseball game without a beer commercial? Even if you go to the game, there are going to be advertisements on the walls.

Because it's hard to realize this is serious stuff masked by humor and casual advertising, adults can help by informing their kids about the dangers of drugs and explain that these famous people are only doing the commercials to make money, and you can't believe everything you see and hear.

— David, 17

■ ■ ■

Unfortunately, many adults take drugs. They don't try to stop drug abuse because they don't want to have to stop.

— Josh, 9

Whenever the subject of drugs comes up, you can hear many parents saying how their child would never do anything like that or how they themselves never did it as a child. You can also hear them preaching to their kids about how it is wrong.

The only thing you never hear about is how drunk "Mark's dad" came home last night or how high "Sally's mom" got at that last party. Many people think that kids discover drugs on their own or just take them to be cool. The truth is that many kids who are drug abusers today picked it up from their own parents.

Kids all over this country are receiving mixed messages. What is a kid supposed to think when his or her mother, who has told them time and time again not to drink and drive, gets a DWI? — Nikki, 15

My most important lesson is not to drink peppermint schnapps, because I get grounded too long. It is not hard to get it because my dad always gets it and I buy it from him. If my mom catches me drinking it, it's bad news. — Boy, 12

My parents do stuff I absolutely hate. I don't mean stuff like make me do dishes, clean my room, watch my brother or sister, or anything like that. My parents smoke pot. I hate it. I can't stand smoke. It makes my eyes burn and makes me so mad.

Something else that makes me mad is when they smoke, it's at dinner or when we are all in the living room.

I am gonna get the guts one day to tell them to quit or they will have one less daughter to worry about. Nobody knows except my best friend and the support group that I'm in. They don't take the hint to stop even though my friend's mom and dad were arrested for smoking and then they went to jail for a while. They still smoke. This summer, I hope to move in with my friend with my brother and sister because I don't think it's a good environment for them to grow up in. — Girl, 14

My father used to be a drug addict and I saw what it did to him. There's no way I'd ever touch that stuff. I suppose a lot of other kids haven't seen something like that so they don't know what they are getting into. If they knew, they wouldn't try it. — Boy, 16

I wonder how many kids have been taking drugs and their parents are the only ones who don't know. The signs are all there, but it's like parents are totally blind to them.

— Rachel, 15

I am a recovering drug addict and alcoholic. I started taking drugs and drinking after being sexually abused by a neighbor man when I was thirteen. I wanted to cover up my insecure and ashamed feelings, and drugs covered these feelings very well. I also used drugs and alcohol because my mom did and I felt unloved by her. My dad was always working and never home, and I thought it was because he hated me.

I didn't want to be "cool" by using, but I wanted to feel loved and accepted, and when I was high or drunk I could pretend I was anyone I wanted to be, and I felt better for a while. I was suicidal. I lied, cheated, stole, and manipulated anyone I could. My life was hell.

I ended up in a drug treatment center. They saved my life.

I am a changed person. I am clean and sober and honest. I actually care about other people and me. I know many people who have died from what I managed to live through.

There is a lot that parents can do to prevent drug use and abuse. Parents can talk to children about how serious drug use is, even experimentation. Parents can let children know they are loved by saying, "I love you," by giving hugs and spending time with children. Parents can be honest and open, and if a parent suspects drug use, don't assume, *ask!* These simple things could have changed my life when I first started using, and these kinds of things did change my life when I got sober.

— Kevin, 17

The biggest thing in my life which I regret thus far has got to be getting a DWI. I have only had my license for about a year. As a result of my DWI arrest, I won't have it again until I turn eighteen. That really sucks.

I don't regret losing my license as much as I do losing the respect of my parents and peers. I am the number one kid in my junior class as far as academics go. I'm sure that I surprised a lot of people by getting a DWI.

I am also on the wrestling team at my school. This year was my year to do really well on the team. As a result of my drinking, I was suspended from two weeks of wrestling right during the tournaments. That really hurt my record a lot and I regret letting my teammates down like that.

I was also elected as next year's football captain for my school. I regret the fact that I am now embarrassed to have a conversation with my football coach because he knows about my DWI. It sucks.

Most of all, I regret letting my parents down. I know they never really expected such irresponsible behavior from me. Now they will never fully trust me to do anything on my own again.

The relationship with my girlfriend also suffered to quite an extent as a result of my illegal drinking. I always felt as though I was in complete control, and I regret that I was too bullheaded to listen to her when she told me not to drive home that night.

Sometimes when I really think about it, I regret being such a problem kid for my parents to deal with. I know it's something I could change in the future, but I'll be leaving home for college in about a year and I will never be able to change the things which I have already done.

Now that everything is over and done, I estimated that the DWI conviction along with the damage to my car and the reinstatement fee for my license will all come to a grand total of about $1,000. I regret that also. — Jason, 17

Everybody should try drugs at least once. They build character. They are good for the imagination. I admit that drugs aren't good for you, but our society would like everyone to believe that if you take drugs once, you will die. I've been doing it for four years. I'm not dead. I'm a little strange, but I'm still normal. I have a better memory than most of my friends. Not all my friends do drugs either; I share a locker with a perfectly straight prep. It is not because of "heavy metal" music either because I started using when I listened to country music.

— Boy, teen

I can't believe how some drug dealers get busted one day and are back on the streets the next day. Maybe there shouldn't be bail on drug dealers because they make enough wasting kids' lives to get themselves out of jail hundreds of times.

— Ann, 13

In the small town where I live, I don't think the law-enforcement officials take the matter very seriously. Parties get broken up and everyone is told to go home, but seldom is the punishment more severe than this. School officials react in much the same way. They don't want to get involved so they look the other way. — Debbie, 17

I know there are commercials and clubs, but one of the best ways to keep from taking drugs is to have really good friends that you can trust and that you can tell your problems to, friends that have close to the same feelings as you. — Sarah, 11

Open communication is a key in problem solving. One way in which my family deals with communication and problem solving is through a weekly family council meeting. In our family council meeting, each family member has an opportunity to vent problems and concerns to other family members. We work together, as a unit, to try and support each other.

My parents also meet once a month, privately, with each child in our family. We have a chance to discuss topics such as school, friends, peer pressure, or any area we choose. My parents always let us know that we are loved, and they will support us in our righteous endeavors.

I am grateful for parents who are willing to talk about my problems. My parents are chemically free; therefore, they set an example for me. — Alicia, 16

■ ■ ■

Teach kids not to take drugs by teaching them how to make choices. In my family, we have a question that helps us decide things: Does it contribute to the good of the world or the bad of the world? — Forrest, 9

One of the best ways to combat drug use is to have a strong faith or religion. It doesn't matter whether you are Christian, Jewish, or whatever, but almost all religions teach that life is precious and that no one is better than anyone else. Most of my friends are Christian and I can see these values really help them stay away from drugs. Kids would stop taking drugs if they really felt they didn't need to and religion is one of the best ways to teach that. — Ted, 13

I've never felt pressured to take drugs because I know that I have so much going for me. I get good grades, get along with my family, and I have terrific friends. Why ruin it all? I also value my life considerably more since I had cancer and went through the trauma of chemotherapy. People take life for granted and it is easy to lose it. — Lisa, 14

One of my closest friends was hooked on drugs and ended up committing suicide two years ago because she thought nobody cared. I really feel sorry for her. Her life ended when she was only thirteen years old. For her sake, and other teens, love your children and tell them that you do. — Girl, 13

Preventing drug abuse is something people talk about, but seldom do. Passing out literature is not enough. Yelling at kids is not enough. We kids and parents have to teach each other. Adults can't help if we won't listen. We can't help if adults won't listen. It's a two-way street from here on. — Jennifer, 15

BELIEFS AND WONDERINGS

GOD

I believe in God because He gave me my dog and He helps us with math. — Ashley, 6

AT AN EARLY age, most kids begin wondering about human origin and purpose and ask the question that inevitably follows: Is there a God? Their questioning is well worth listening to, for when children express their existential intimations and ponderings, their certainty and their bewilderment, we all learn more about what it means to be human.

When asked if they believe in a God or other spiritual force or power, children's responses range from profound doubt to profound faith. Some children paint rapturous portraits of a benevolent creator while others offer anguished tirades about a God responsible only for suffering and despair. Many frame their beliefs in the language of formal religious doctrine; others share deeply personal musings.

A minority are certain no God exists now and never did, but for the majority God is real whether it be the Christian or Judaic God, Buddha, Krishna, Allah, the Goddess, or other spiritual forms. Most frequently God is depicted as the traditional fatherly figure in flowing robes presiding over the universe from a heavenly throne. The younger children especially imagine God as human, most like a child's father or grandfather, sometimes sporting a handlebar mustache or clad in the latest fashions. A substantial number of kids envision God quite differently, using he/she/it combinations to describe female, male/female, or genderless deities. God for some is Black, for one it's a blonde woman in her thirties, for another God is all colors combined. A few see God as a faceless robot, or a swirling vapor or force. One twelve-year-old boy writes that God appears to him in animal form in his dreams. For a young girl passionately enamored of horses God can be nothing less than a bay thoroughbred stallion.

Most believe as they do because that's how they've been raised. They cite parental example and years of churchgoing as the foundation for their faith. Often a grandmother also looms large in a child's spiritual development by teaching about prayer or taking a child to church when the parents don't. Many youngsters acknowledge that had they been raised in a different family with different beliefs, they might believe differently. Yet, some believe unquestioningly that their family's God is the only true god.

Nature provides proof of God's existence for some. For others faith is rooted in a need to believe that someone or something is in charge, giving meaning to life and comfort in death. Younger children especially wrestle with the classic dilemma: If God made us, who made God?

A startling number believe they've been the benefactors of God's miracles. Kids of all ages are convinced they survived or surmounted a difficult experience only because of God's direct intervention. One is certain God cured her allergies, another believes in God because her cat, a nonswimmer, didn't drown when thrown into the pool. Several believe because they've escaped serious injury in car accidents; one because he moved at just the right moment during a storm so a falling tree didn't crush him; a couple because they found their way out of the woods when they were lost. Their faith is founded in occurrences as profound as their father surviving combat in Vietnam and as trivial as their being able to do just one more pull-up in gym.

The natures of the Gods they describe range from vindictive and terrifying to loving, merciful, and kind, to decidedly imperfect. Several assert that God's primary purpose is to be the conscience that guides them on moral issues and decisions. One former drug user credits God for getting and keeping him straight. For the majority, God matters most because it is a "forever friend." Youngsters turn to God when parents won't listen or yell too much or when they feel their young lives are out of control. God, unlike other forces in their lives, is utterly dependable and makes them feel safe. One young child believes God exists because someone has to guard children who are home alone after school.

Just as many adults do, young people ask, if God is real, then why is there so much ugliness in the world; why do murder, rape, AIDS, pollution, racism, war, and death exist? Who or what would have created a world this confusing and full of suffering? The death of a grandparent or a parent, or the suicide of a young cousin, can mean the end of faith altogether. A teenage boy writes, "When I'm sitting in the juvenile detention center, I pray, pray, and pray for things to come out my way, but it doesn't seem to work. Now when I'm this far down, I feel that there is no way there could possibly be a God."

If God exists, some nonbelievers write, surely someone could have proved it by now. Why, they ask, would a God powerful enough to create the world be unwilling to reveal itself and put to rest everyone's questions about the nature of God and the universe? For some, their minds boggle as they attempt to reconcile evolution and dinosaurs with Genesis. Many give up on God when their prayers go unanswered.

Some young people, especially teenagers, renounce God precisely because of the pressure to believe. They use words like "brainwashing" and "drilled into" to describe how religion has been forced into them from early ages. Several say that during those years no one asked them what they truly believed and that few if any adults even would entertain their questions. Denim, 15, writes, "It's hard to believe in God because if you believe in Him, society says you aren't supposed to question, doubt, or disbelieve anything religious. It's hard, too, to understand why God does things like take mommies and daddies or cause pain or create awful disease, but society speaks again: 'God has a reason, don't question Him.' Why not? If He has a reason, why can't we ask what it is?"

A questioning thirteen-year-old ends her piece this way, "To write this essay took a lot of heart. I really feel like I've betrayed my religion, my family, and myself." Another teen writes, "My grandparents are Roman Catholics and if they ever found out I didn't believe in a God (their God), they would disown me and accuse me of being a 'devil worshipper.' I think that's ignorant."

For many the doubts and questions eventually transform the religion of their parents into a spirituality of their own. One perceives a yearning for adults, particularly parents, to listen, understand, and maybe even to share their own doubts with their children as they try to navigate their spiritual journey.

Youngsters are capable of a wondrous array of thoughts on the existence and nature of God. Whether they write joyously of a God who enriches their lives or vehemently pronounce their skepticism, their expressions are a testament to the personal nature of any human's search for meaning.

■ ■ ■

I do believe in a God and this is what she looks like. She is tall and has long brown hair and wears glasses and always wears some sort of different kind of look each day. She is nice and cares for everyone and takes care of the homeless that come to her home when they die. She lives in the mist above the clouds. It is very pretty up there, and she can look down over the people. I would love to live there.

She flies like an angel and has mystical powers. She knows more than anyone in the world. — Emily, 8

■ ■ ■

I want God to look tough, like a weightlifter. I would also want him to be nice like a mother. — Joe, 10

God's qualities are that he's tall with brown hair with a little white in it, nice, caring, loves everybody, and is interesting, kind of like my dad. — Elisabeth, 8

God doesn't have to be a white man. God could be a black woman or a piece of broken rock or something that somebody decides to worship. God could be the sun or the moon. God even could be an arrowhead, totem pole, or werewolf, even a dead cat. — Faye, 16

I believe in God, but not in the god that we learn about in church or in other religions. I believe in the god in yourself that makes you act and look the way you do. — Reeve, 9

■ ■ ■

I think of God as a pal. He likes rock music, big stereos, and skateboarding. That's because I think that what you imagine God to be is what he is. — Ryan, 13

I believe that there is a God and Jesus and if anyone isn't born again and have Jesus in their heart they, or even you, will be doomed to hell. Many of you, I'm sure, will probably say something like, "Why should I go to heaven, none of my friends will be there," and then you might even laugh. You may say anything for a joke, but heaven and hell are both real, not a joke.

I want all Baptists that don't believe in speaking in other tongues to hear this. I believe in it and it is not a doctrine of Satan, but a gift from God. — Brent, 10

■ ■ ■

I believe in God because I am a Christian. He made good people, bad people, and stupid people. He made rabbits, dogs, and lunch meat. He made everything. And that is why I love him so much. — Eric, 10

Just look in the mirror once and tell yourself that you were an accidental fusing of amino acids and try to believe it.

— Kerry, 17

If you lived on a farm like I do, you would know there is a God. By the way he controls the weather, the growth of crops, and the miracle of birth, he proves it to me every day. Who else would send sunshine after a storm, supply us with food for hunger, and water for thirst?

If you could see a newborn animal search for food immediately after birth, you would know there is a God, too. My God is beside me and the farm every single day. Who else could do that besides God? No one! — Layton, 16

Yes, there is a God. He has a beard and looks over us. There is a big gate and when you die the gate opens and you can become an angel and pray all the time. God has this TV screen and sees if someone sins. He has a TV screen because the angels gave it to him on his birthday. The screen is in the workroom. It sits up in the clouds. — Rebecca, 8

■ ■ ■

I believe in God so much that I wish I could touch him.
— Kierstin, 8

People often ask what God looks like and I could tell them. I see God several times every day, every time I look into a mirror. My friends think I'm joking when I comment on my divine omnipotence because I am joking. But I am truly God. I'm not God in the sense that I'm a supreme being or power who controls the events that shape people's lives. Rather, I am God just as all of us are God. God is not a cognitive spirit that dictates life on Earth. God is an essence within all of us. That essence is what we pray will aid us and give us strength. That essence can appear as a small caring gesture or as a massive movement for human improvement. God can appear at any time in any positive way. I am essentially a positive person and so I am God. — Paul, 16

The God I believe in is like a warm sensation that you get when you open a Christmas gift. — Tracy, 13

If God were a human being, he would probably be very polite to others. — Toni, 9

One reason I believe in God is in some way I can feel him in my bones. It feels like how some people can feel the weather in their bones—I can feel God in my bones. — Lindsey, 11

■ ■ ■

Many people think I'm ugly, but to God I'm pretty because he made me in his image. — Girl, 11

■ ■ ■

God had so much love in him he had to make us to get some love out. — Rachel, 9

You can always talk to your God and tell him your thoughts and feelings. . . . It's kind of like having your own personal, invisible psychiatrist. — Angie, 13

I think of God as my friend and I talk to him a lot when something is bothering me. You can say anything to him and he will listen with all his heart. When I picture him I think of him as a grandfather. He is old and wise, but very strong. But it's his hands that are his most striking feature. They are leathery but soft. His hands are strong and can hold you tight at a moment's notice. God's voice is strong and sturdy and will soothe you right down to the bottom of your soul. He wears a white robe with many shining layers, so if you are cold he takes one off and covers you with it. But what I love the most is his heart. It is so big and warm that it has enough love to love each and every person on earth. — Elisabeth, 14

When I have a problem I go to my parents, but if I have a problem I can't tell my parents, I go to God. — Joe, 12

■ ■ ■

Sometimes I think of God as a 911 God. When I need help, I call him and he helps out. — Laura, 10

I believe in God because when my parents got a divorce it felt like I wasn't all alone. God was helping me to get through it. — Pam, 14

I believe in my guardian angel. I think that some people don't have a guardian angel, like for example, a hooker does not have a guardian angel. — Boy, 10

One time I asked God to not send my dad into heaven. He must have said he should be on earth for a couple more years because my dad is still alive! — Shawn, 9

I do believe in God. I feel that if he actually does exist I can see my dad again. So I see God as a hope. — Laura, 12

■ ■ ■

My dad's aunt died and my dad cried, but he got better so I said to myself, "It must be God making him feel better."
— Alice, 7

When my great-grandma died I prayed and asked if she was all right and if she was to let it be sunny for one week. And it was sunny for one week. — Jenny, 12

At my house praying isn't necessary at supper. The only time we pray is when our relatives are over. — Lisa, 11

I like to go to church because it leaves me with a good, holy feeling when I'm done. But my father is a Lutheran, my mother is a Catholic, and my stepmother is a Methodist, so I end up going to a lot of different churches, even though I myself am a Catholic. My dad says that Methodist and Lutheran are better religions than Catholic because they give their people more freedom and that may be true (I'm not sure), but the Catholic church always gives me a more holy feeling than the Methodist or Lutheran church. I usually end up going to the Methodist church with my father and stepmother, though, because no matter what church I go to, it's still church and it's better than not going at all. A lot better. — Beth, 11

I don't think God wanted the world to be made up of so many religions. I think he wanted one religion so it would be efficient. — Joe, 10

Religion has never really been pushed on me by my parents, but it has by my grandmother who is a strict Baptist. I remember the Easter when I was nine and I went to church with her. While in Sunday school the teacher asked me if I had ever been saved. Not knowing what that meant I innocently said, "No." The next thing I knew I was up in front of the class taking Jesus as my personal savior and then being knocked to the floor! I am afraid that this incident has discouraged me from being Baptist. — Dana, 13

Goddess and God are things you must find inside yourself and for yourself. No one should have gods forced upon them.
— Penny, 14

I love God, I really do. It's just that every Sunday my parents shove it down my throat. I mean well, but Mom and Dad feel that if you don't get all spruced up, you're not a true Christian. I know Mom and Dad love me, but if they really think I love going to a place where you have to sing a hymn that has words not even the best English scholar could figure out, they're wrong. To sum it up, I like God. It's just that worshipping him isn't all it's cracked up to be. — Kurt, 12

I believe in God but sometimes I get confused. The one thing I have trouble with is evolution. The main reason is because I always watch those shows about how we started out as monkeys and evolved into humans. Now the big question is did God make monkeys, not like them, and change them into humans? Or did the monkeys just appear and start changing into humans? We may never know.

One other thing I have a problem with is how the Earth was

formed. Did God just make the Earth or is one of those theories, like the Big Bang Theory, right? Also, if he made the Earth, why do the continents keep moving? Does God get bored at looking at the same shapes for millions and millions of years? Perhaps he didn't make the Earth at all.

I do believe in God, but I still have some questions about his work. — Stacy, 13

When I even start to think, "What if there isn't a God?" I always just say, "Slow down." I have to believe in God or I would be scared, really scared. — Julie, 11

I believe in God because I want to. It is too depressing not to. — James, 11

I sort of believe in Jesus because I've read the Bible. But for all we know, some sort of wacko could have written that.

— David, 10

I often am uncertain as to whether or not there really is a God. When I sit down and think about it I have my doubts, but whenever I need help desperately I seem to ask God for assistance and he usually comes through. So I guess that in my heart I believe in God, but I'm unsure in my brain.

— Richard, 18

I still don't know where God lives. Why doesn't he/she live down here? — Rory, 10

Is there a God? From personal experience, I have absolutely no idea. Every Saturday morning I pray in a synagogue and help younger children, I almost never sin and I try very hard in school, but I still have family problems, I still am persecuted against for being a Jew, and since I'm small, people often threaten to hurt me just to make them feel better. So I certainly haven't seen any sign of a God.

But, say there is a God. Why are "good" people dying? And what about the Holocaust? Why were millions of innocent people burned and gassed? I think what might have happened is God created life, watched over us for a few years, and just drifted off and left when he found out his little world wasn't perfect. But that's not fair!! And there's nothing we can do about it. — Mike, 14

I no longer believe in him. Three years ago he, meaning God, took the most important person in my life. That person was my father. The thing that bothers me the most is that my father was only forty-two years old when God stole him from me. I realize that everybody has to go at some time, but my father had his whole life ahead of him. Maybe in a couple of years I will start to believe in God once again, but for now, I do not believe in the so-called hero called God. — Boy, 15

I believe in Satan. If I believe in Satan, I have to believe in the Biblical God, but I believe in Satan more. I believe in Satan because I believe in evil. I believe that there are no "good" people on earth. When the world comes to an end, there will be a battle between good and evil, and evil will triumph. All people have done evil. Therefore, there is literally no such thing as good. Satan is a dark, powerful god with powers beyond the wildest imagination. He can torture souls for eternity and destroy lives. He's not picky about his prisoners. He takes anybody. I believe in dark powers and Satan. If evil doesn't overpower good, I'll be sent to hell anyway. — Boy, 17

I am mad at God sometimes when he is not helping us to save our earth. Our air is bad, our neighborhoods are becoming full of crimes. People are afraid to open a window at night and they don't leave their homes because they are afraid. God could stop that with a snap of a finger, but he doesn't. Why?

— Nathan, 14

■ ■ ■

When my sister fell through the ice of a creek we all prayed she would be okay, but she wasn't okay. She died. So Jesus makes me think he is not always going to help people.

— Carie, 14

I would like to believe in God, but I think my friends would make fun of me. They ain't into him and he ain't hip no more.

— Boy, 16

People need someone to answer to, someone who has all the answers, even if they only exist in their mind. I am jealous of people who are capable of having faith in what seems to me to be a fairy tale. — Cera, 16

I don't consider myself an atheist nor do I consider myself a highly religious person. I consider myself confused.

— Josh, 15

DEATH

When people die their soul turns into a star so everyone can look up and say how beautiful they are. — Brigette, 15

KIDS THINK ABOUT death when grandparents or pets die, a sibling commits suicide, a mother miscarries, a classmate is killed in an accident. They worry about death when they hear too much about AIDS and murder or when a war breaks out or a plane crashes. They wonder about death when they lie all alone in the dark at night. Once in a while they even contemplate it while they're blowing up anthills with firecrackers.

In part because we rarely talk about death in our society, many kids say that questions about death—why it occurs, if life after death exists or if it doesn't, why not—rank among the most difficult to consider.

Why do people die? The young people's most frequent response is population control. They say that the earth's resources would be taxed to the limit in short order if death didn't occur. The economy would be shattered, the environment would be ravaged, and the number of homeless would skyrocket. In addition, no young people could get jobs because they would be competing with adults with a thousand years of experience. They believe that everyone must die to give other people a chance at life. Many envision life without death as terrifying; they imagine people becoming increasingly decrepit, cranky, and ill at ease as they age forever.

Some see death as necessary to ease people's suffering from illness and to spare people from the boredom of infinite life. Others simply see it as the natural order of things; it's as simple as, "Because God made it that way." Very few, however, cite original sin as the cause of human mortality.

A surprising number suggest that people die because they want to, not that they commit suicide, but that they grow so weary, lonely, or bored that they lose their desire to live. "People die of old age when their skin gets wrinkled and their heart stops. The heart stops because it has too much pain," writes Jon, 9.

Without death, the world wouldn't progress, say a few. If people didn't die, the world would be saddled with the same leaders, the same thinkers, the same tired systems forever. New ideas and innovative solutions to problems would never occur; death is what keeps the world vital. People die because they've completed a mission, write some. That mission can be saving someone's life, raising thirteen children, even dying so loved ones will bond together and appreciate each other more.

For many of the more literal minds, the reason for death can be articulated only in terms of the causes of death. Kids say people die because of aging, disease, or accidents. It's not uncommon that youngsters also include shooting, stabbing, drunk drivers, and kidnapping among their reasons for why people die.

A huge majority believe in some kind of afterlife, with most describing a version of heaven and/or variations on reincarnation. They must believe life goes on, many say, or what purpose would life serve? They propose that life is too hard and too much work not to have a reward at the end.

For some, heaven is the standard picture of clouds, harps, golden gates, and singing angels draped in white, but for far more, heaven is a uniquely individual vision. Especially for young children, heaven is their wish list come true. It's a place with no bullies, no homework, no teasing, no bossing, no toothaches. Junk food and cute boys abound and the stuffed animals can talk. No parents get divorced. No one poaches elephants. In heaven you can meet your heroes—Davy Crockett or Babe Ruth or a former Hollywood star

—and they're no better than you are. Private swimming pools, bright colors, and diamonds are everywhere. In heaven, you can't get grounded and God is always available for a conference and will comfort you if you're homesick. For many, heaven beats even Disney World, the state fair, and the local shopping mall combined for a good time.

The older kids generally have a more subdued vision of heaven, a place that's more a state of mind than a fantasyland. "If you ask a three-year-old what heaven is, she'll say things like bubblegum trees or soda fountains and marshmallow steps," writes Erin. "When you ask me as a thirteen-year-old, I say that there's no hurt, no pain. Everyone's equal. It's very peaceful." For older kids, heaven is a place of no regrets, no mistakes, and no loneliness.

Regardless of their age, most youngsters say that the best part of heaven would be reunions with dead loved ones, particularly grandparents and pets. They describe idyllic towns in heaven in which families are together, sitting in cozy kitchens, talking, laughing, and reveling in one another. They look forward to meeting ancestors and talking about how life was way back when.

Very few mention hell, and if they do, they often say they don't believe it exists or that almost no one goes there. Even fewer mention purgatory or limbo. Instead a few suggest that heaven itself has a variety of levels to which people can aspire. Although the highest level of heaven is most enjoyable, no one in any level suffers.

Reincarnation enjoys wide acceptance among young people. Some believe reincarnation must occur for the same reason death must—overpopulation. If people aren't returned to something, heaven will become uncomfortably overcrowded. One of the most common beliefs is that when a person dies the soul enters a new-born baby. Another common view is that you can be reincarnated into animals, either one you choose or one thrust upon you depending upon how you lived your life, or even into things such as a lake, pine tree, or baseball. Some believe reincarnation can be punitive—a white racist, for instance, probably will become a black person in his next life. One group believes a person is reincarnated only once, another that people actually live millions of lives until they've experienced every possibility in life or corrected all their mistakes. Reincarnated souls are transported to other planets or galaxies and maybe even materialize in alternate dimensions. One believes when people die, their souls soar to a spot in their star sign.

Among the reasons for belief in reincarnation are personal *déjà vu* experiences, movies and TV programs that present it as a possibility, and a sense many have that pets with which they have a special relationship are really dead parents or friends come back to life. Large numbers relate experiences that seem to substantiate the reincarnation theory, including Jefferson, 10: "My great-grandmother spoke about reincarnation and that if there was such a thing she would want to come back as a goldfinch. The day after she died, there was a goldfinch sitting on Aunt Sally's windowsill! Sure made Aunt Sally wonder about it! Was it just a coincidence?"

For some the afterlife must exist because they or people they love have had experiences with spirits. They tell of dead fathers or grandmothers appearing in their dreams and describing heaven. They've heard stories from friends and relatives encountering ghosts in their homes or experiencing mysterious pranks. They've seen pictures fall off walls at funerals for no apparent reason. Some recount stories of people who have just died appearing to loved ones or even to themselves far from the site of their death.

A striking theme in the young people's writing is choice. Large numbers believe that after death a person can choose for himself whether he stays in heaven for a day or a year or forever; is reincarnated sooner or later, once or twice or eternally; becomes a guardian angel for a baby or loved one; exists in a particular form in a particular place and time. Another common opinion is expressed by LeAnn, 17: "Life after death is what the mind believes it to be. Those who say 'There is no life after death,' will not have life after death. Their disbelief has made it impossible." She is one of many who believe after death you experience whatever you believed you would.

A small minority believe life simply ends and nothingness or eternal blackness ensues. Some describe graphically the deterioration of the body into dust, others propose that the end is merely a long, dreamless sleep.

Among the children's responses are many from kids grieving

over the death of loved ones. Death to them is no abstract concept, but instead a daily reality that leaves them puzzled and in pain. "When someone close to you like Grandpa dies, it hurts. You feel like you want to die, too," writes Jeanne, 12. Although some are comforted by parents assuring them that death ended a loved one's suffering, that paradise is real, that a reunion will inevitably occur, most discover that the pain remains for a long while.

Regardless of how personally comfortable or uncomfortable we adults are with death, we need to understand that our children are aware of and often perplexed by it. For example, when my youngest brother died, my three-and-a-half-year-old nephew viewed the body in a half-opened casket that revealed my brother from his waist up. It wasn't until several years later at another funeral that my sister became aware of what had affected her son most about my brother's death. He had wondered for years why when a person dies, people cut off his legs. It's a gruesome picture and not one that could have been anticipated. But it's a reminder that children observe and wonder not just about the life around them, but about the death around them as well.

How youngsters as well as adults feel about death is succinctly summed up by Ross, 11. He writes, "I wish I really knew if there is life after death or not. And I wish I could find out without dying."

■ ■ ■

If people didn't die, the world would be crowded. Then all your relatives would have to move in with you. — Ann, 10

People die because it is a test for relatives and friends on how they overcome their sadness. The way they overcome their sadness judges if they go to heaven or not. — Lance, 9

If we all lived forever, then love would not be as valuable as it is today. If we know that no one can leave us, we will all take each other for granted. — Leann, 17

If no one ever died it wouldn't be any fun. Everyone would have done everything, seen everything, and been everywhere. There would be nothing left to do. — Matt, 11

People die because their body is too old and has to stop working and that makes death. Some people are afraid to die. But down inside you your body says, "I don't want to work for you anymore." Then you die. — Ali, 9

When I start to think of death, I think of confusion. Why does a twelve-year-old die before a twenty-year-old? Why have some sixteen-year-olds never experienced the death of a loved one and yet I've experienced seven? Why did two of my loved ones die within six months? Why do some people get a second chance at life and others none? Why do some people get a warning that death is near and others leave the world without having any warning that their time had expired? These are just some of the many questions I have that confuse me.

— Rachel, 16

Why do people have to die is one of the saddest questions you could ask someone. Especially me since my dad died when I was in fifth grade. He was very special to me because he and I had a special relationship that no one else in our family had (except for maybe him and my mother). I know what caused his death, but I don't know why he had to die. I probably never will know why either. Something I do know is he didn't want to die and that's the important thing, to me at least.

Before he died our family never went to church. Now every Sunday we go to church and Sunday school. I never before believed in anything like heaven or life after death. Now I believe that somewhere, I don't know where, but somewhere, he's looking at me and hopefully thinking something like, "That's my daughter." I hope he's proud. — Clarissa, 11

The time I think about death the most is when I hear my friends talking about *if* they grow up instead of *when* they grow up. — Elizabeth, 12

This month we had to put our dog to sleep and I haven't been able to concentrate very well. In spelling I get words wrong because I miss Buffy. And when my teacher tells us directions, I have to ask someone else for the directions. I guess all I have to do is wait and maybe I won't feel so sad about my dog, Buffy. I really miss Buffy. — Shelly, 10

People have to die because if we didn't, God would get lonely. — Keith, 12

■ ■ ■

People have to die because death makes everyone equal.
— Chelsea, 15

■ ■ ■

I believe in life after death because I think it's like a Nintendo game. Once you die, you still have another life to live.
— Sarah, 11

I do believe in life after death because I heard someone walking upstairs at one A.M. and it wasn't my parents. — Jenny, 9

■ ■ ■

The only reason I would want to die is because I would be able to walk through the golden gates to heaven. I would see the house I have now, only my room would be clean.
— Jocelyn, 11

Heaven seems like a nice place with a cloud floor and it would be good to see your dead friends and relatives. There are golden gates and on them there is a sign that says HEAVEN written in diamonds. There would be a rock shop and a huge toy store with millions of free toys. There would be a malt shop and a bakery that sells Rice Krispie bars. There would be big shopping centers just like on earth and for Christmas Jesus would dress up as Santa Claus.

You would make lots of friends and you would share a house with a pool with them. You would have your own horse and dogs and cats, too. They would be the most tamest pets you have ever had. Your pool would have a slide and a diving board, and if you got lonely up there, you could still look down on your family and friends from the sky. — Emily, 10

An example of heaven is when kids have birthday parties. Kids have a lot of fun. They don't fight. They just enjoy being together. This is what heaven is like. — Cole, 11

I think you wake up in a garden full of flowers. Then you feel good, you really feel great. You're young again and everybody else is, too. Then your mom, dad, or pets that died come and take you to eternal life. Your home is on a cloud. *Wait!!!!* You can fly and there's peace forever. — John, 9

Up in heaven you can watch all the sports games and you can giggle at people who are in a big mess. — Drew, 11

I believe that when people die only half of their soul goes to Heaven. The other half stays with you and your loved ones.

— Shannon, 11

■ ■ ■

When you die I think you go to heaven. When you get there you will be the center attraction. Then you will go to a great big mansion with a pool shaped like the first letter of your name. — Lynette, 10

Life is really great, but when people die it is really hard to take. But I believe in life after death. You get put in a coffin sorta like a nice, cozy bed. Then Jesus comes with a key and opens it and takes you. You both soar through the air up to heaven. You get there and it is the most beautiful thing in the whole world. Then you see your grandma and grandpa and they both greet you.

It feels like you're walking on air. Your eyes are going crazy. Then you walk down God's Street! It is so beautiful that you just feel like a bear that sees honey. There is a waterfall and so many houses. And there are so many people like Elvis Presley and more.

Then God tells you the rules. They aren't very hard. Then he takes you to your house. It is so wonderful that you feel like you're home for good. Everything is made out of clouds. Even the toilet. And then God says, "Peace be with you forever." And then God goes and waits for the next one.

— Christopher, 11

Heaven is a place of great beauty. There are different levels for each period in time like Roman, Medieval, and today.

— Rob, 9

I believe in life after death because I believe Jesus is still alive in heaven.

The reason I believe in Jesus is because when I was eleven years old, one night we couldn't find our cat, so we just went to bed. So the next night at the same time our cat disappeared, our dog disappeared. I went to bed crying. That night I prayed, God, would you please find our cat and dog and put them on our doorstep in the morning before my mom leaves for work? The next morning before my mom left for work, the dog and the cat were sitting on the doorstep.

And that is why I believe there is life after death. — Jill, 12

■ ■ ■

When people die they go to heaven and they have nice, nice people that make tacos. — J.J., 9

In heaven it will be very peaceful and people wear white and they're very nice and they act like ladies and gentlemen and they use very nice manners. You will just be as happy as you ever could be. You would see God and Jesus every day and you would say hello and they would say, "Good day, young man." — Nick, 10

I'd like to go up to heaven because I could make snow.
— Isaac, 11

When you die you go to heaven and heaven will be a beautiful white palace surrounded by soccer fields. I also believe that when you die you have the choice of going straight to heaven or staying on Earth for a short period before you go to heaven to fool around, scare people, or see your family. But, however, if you are bad when you are alive, you go to hell. — Peter, 9

I don't really believe in heaven, but my mom wants me to, so I try. — Girl, 11

You can call me weird, but I believe in reincarnation. See, when I was nine years old, one of my old friends died. She was about seventy-two. When I was about 10, I bought a fish. It was a beta. I talked to the beta and it reminded me of my old friend. — Lynette, 10

I believe that when a human being dies, he leaves his mortal shell behind him. Then the spirit goes into a bough of a spruce tree, the eye of a wolf, or another creature of nature.

I also believe a human child is born without a spirit or soul. Then later in life a child has to earn his spirit. What I believe happens is that the child looks right into the eye of his future spirit. Then the spirit leaps from its hiding place into the body of the child.

Then when he dies, it starts all over again like a never-ending cycle for all of eternity. — Tony, 13

I'm guessing that when you die you see God and choose your family, eye color, hair color, and if you want to be a boy or girl. Then you are born and by the time you're old enough to talk, you forget. Have you ever noticed how you can't remember when you were little by the time you are older? If you ask me, I don't think that's just a coincidence! — Samantha, 12

I had a sister but she died. I was not alive, but I think it would have been scary. She was just a little baby. Maybe I was her. I would not have been alive if she did not die. — Holli, 9

I used to think that my grandpa would come back, but who knows what he will come back as. I wish he would come back as my grandfather again. — Rose, 12

■ ■ ■

I do not believe in reincarnation because I could be Elvis and that would be weird. — Josh, 11

My grandma died. I had a dream she came back. I thought I opened my eyes and she was there. I think she might be living in France as a little kid. — Anne, 9

When you die, you're dead, as in will never be seen again ever again by anyone or anything anywhere. — Seth, 13

I am scared to die. It's probably a dark, dark world. You don't feel, smell, or hear anything. You have no idea what your child or friends may be doing. You're gone forever, even your thoughts. Even if you go to heaven, it would be scary.

— Katie, 9

What I think happens to people when they die is they wither up and the bugs eat them and they turn into bones. Millions of years later that person will turn into oil and never be seen again. — Kavon, 11

When I think of death I think of heaven and Katie. Katie is my sister who died when I was only one and a half years old. Although I never met her, I miss her. I guess it's because I have a clear picture of what she would be like.

Mom says that she was a bubbly, cheerful person. She would always bounce around chattering to herself. Mom said Katie would stand in front of my playpen and make faces at me until I nearly died laughing.

I guess if I knew why she died it would be easier to accept. I suppose God took her home to him to keep her from harm. That's fine with me because I wouldn't want her to have to live on earth with all its problems. I'm glad she was spared from having to be here when Mom and Dad divorced. When she died, everything was happy and I'm glad it was that way.

I look forward to dying. I'm not scared at all. I know God will come and take me home. There I can see Grandpa S. and best of all, I can finally meet Katie. There in heaven we both can be glorified and I'll have all eternity to be with her.

— Janeen, 12

On June 15, 1989, my mother was on her way to work. A semitruck broadsided her knocking her truck sixty-three feet across the highway. The semitruck had run a stop sign. My mother was killed instantly.

My regret is that it seems that I might have been able to save her. What if I talked to her just for ten more seconds that morning? That's all it would have taken. What if I would have had breakfast with her? Again, ten seconds either way would have saved her life.

There's so many possibilities it blew my mind when I thought about it, and they seemed to all come down to me, and there's always that sense of guilt. I was the only one home with her that morning. I should have been able to do something. I'll always have a feeling in the bottom of my heart, I could have saved her. — Chad, 15

I remember looking at my grandpa at the wake. He looked like he was breathing. I said to my dad, "Look, he's breathing." He said, "I thought that, too, but it's only because we love him so much that we wish he was." — Nicki, 15

When I was about eight my grandpa committed suicide. When I found out, the first thing I asked was if Grandpa would go to heaven. My mom said yes, but I overheard some relatives saying that people who commit suicide always go to hell. I didn't believe it then and I still don't now. My grandpa had his faults, but he was a kind person who believed in God.
— Girl, 14

When my close friend died, my parents were not very supportive, I'm not quite sure why, maybe they didn't know that as a child I could experience the terrible pain which occurred with death. If only they, as adults, would have sat down, talked to me and tried to explain to me what and where exactly my friend had disappeared to. Maybe only if they would have given me a single hug and let me cry, it would have made things better.

If I could have one wish about what adults could do better, it would be to help children deal with death easier.
— Ericka, 17

I feel very sad when I hear a friend or family member dies. I really think that God must really want them up in heaven

with him. But sometimes I get very mad and scared. I think that maybe one day God will just take everyone I care about.
— Christina, 12

■ ■ ■

When loved ones die I think everyone hurts. And when people say they're too old to cry, they don't really mean it 'cause they cry inside. — Kristi, 10

Thinking about death makes me want to go out and do everything I've never done before my time is up. Everyone should treasure their lives for the short time they have because all lives are limited and all living things will die. — Rachel, 12

18

WAR AND PEACE

Peace is good. War is very, very rough. Peace is quiet. War
is noisy. Peace is nice. I wish there was peace and never war.
— Katri, 8

FOR CÉNTURIES HUMANS have wrestled with issues of war and
peace, pondering whether human nature is such that genuine
world peace might ever be attainable. Today's youngsters, who are
well aware of the amount of conflict in the world, also wonder if
their generation or any future generations will ever live in a peaceful world. Their concerns and hopes are frequently reflected in
"Mindworks."

For instance, in the earlier years of "Mindworks," kids commonly
wrote of their fear of nuclear annihilation, a fear that has diminished substantially in recent years. When the United States invaded
Grenada in 1983 and Panama in 1989, kids wrote of their fear and
concern; when more than two hundred Marines were killed in
Beirut in 1983, they wrote to express their sorrow. Many write
about war because they have fathers who served in Vietnam and
grandfathers who saw action in Korea or World War II. Some of
those children continue to pay the price of those wars by having
fathers, grandfathers, or uncles whose war experiences left them
shattered and incapable of participating fully in children's lives.

Many students from Southeast Asia frequently write about war because they and their families lived through one.

When "Mindworks" asked directly, "Given human nature, do you believe peace on Earth—a time when there is absolutely no war—is possible?" the timing proved eerily appropriate. The topic was determined in the summer of 1990 and scheduled for publication in February 1991. That meant that the kids were wrestling with the questions of war and peace under the threat of war. They were writing after President Bush set the January 15 deadline for Iraq to vacate Kuwait, but before war broke out in the Persian Gulf.

Perhaps because they were writing under the shadow of impending conflict, a majority of the thousands declare: "World peace? Never." However, given the youngsters' general views on the future, which tend to be pessimistic, even hopeless, it's likely their views would have been nearly the same regardless of the timing.

The Earth will never know peace, they write, because this world and its inhabitants are imperfect; because people are motivated by greed, jealousy, and lust for power, because of everlasting inequities. Besides, at least one lunatic always will surface to wreak havoc for us all, write many.

"I doubt that we can ever be a peaceful world," writes James, 17. "Hatred wells up in the pores of our lives. We hate our neighbors, we hate the people on TV, we hate the lives we lead. It is our nature to hate."

Hundreds describe their own squabbles and battles on the home front as evidence of the inevitability of conflict. If families and friends can't get along, they say, how can we possibly expect strangers from different cultures to? One says peace is unlikely in a world where people fight over parking spaces at Christmas.

"Maybe if the world had one leader and we were all one color, the same religion, and everybody had the same amount of money and the government controlled our minds to think the same thoughts, then we could have total peace," writes Sarah, 14. She's one of thousands who cite intolerance of religious, cultural, and individual diversity as an insoluble cause of war.

For most, world peace means more than the absence of countries at war. Peace occurs, they say, only when racism, divorce, poverty, sexism, crime, and homelessness are eradicated; when drug wars, gang warfare, and environmental destruction are problems of the past.

Those who suggest peace is possible load their essays with words like "miracle," "if only," "I wish." Many believe peace will prevail when all people "come to their senses," love one another, cooperate, and commit themselves to peace no matter what the cost. A couple hope for a magic peace potion or dust that could be liberally spread across the Earth.

The first step to peace is to destroy all weapons, say many, though others wonder what to destroy since almost any object can be used to kill. Others suggest that speeches that can touch even the "cruelest hearts," impassioned letters for peace delivered to people in power and more frequent recitations of the rosary would prompt peace. One recommends combining all the world's religions into one "Super Religion" so everyone would have that in common; another that the whole world vote on which god to believe in—majority rules.

We need more treaties and an antiwar law—anyone who breaks them goes to jail—or maybe we could merge all our countries into one country with one language and two presidents—a man and a woman, suggest some. Several assert that if women had more power in world affairs, war would disappear.

Peace is possible if we destroy leaders like Saddam Hussein, execute criminals, kill prejudiced people, and rocket violent people to different planets, some proclaim. Others say peace will be a reality when humans are replaced by robots or alien life forms. Scores believe peace will come only when God decides it will.

Peace won't occur in their lifetimes, say most, but maybe it will during the lives of their children or in a million years or when the planet explodes. Several say they would decline peace if it were offered—the world would be too boring.

Overall these essays are marked with a great seriousness. Many of those written by children who at the time had loved ones stationed in the Persian Gulf, resonate with anger, fear, and sorrow; others resound with hope. P.J., 10, captures the reality of any war with a P.S. he adds to his essay: "Uncle Jay, please come home, not in a body bag, but in person."

■ ■ ■

Peace will someday be on this world, but like a bird it will fly away because we chase it away. — Mahi, 11

I have a feeling that World War III is coming. I can just feel it coming. I hope not, but I think so. — Steve, 10

I dream a lot about the future, but my most vivid dream is about nuclear war.

I don't know where I am. Suddenly the sky turns red. The farmland is bathed in a strange reddish light. Then it comes— the nuclear bomb. It moves silently, yet it is a horrible silence. It explodes. Power and anger, earth and sky blend and then I, the earth, the universe are gone. — Margit, 11

Missiles, bombs, and guns don't make for good communication. — Annie, 10

My mother and I agree on many subjects, but the possibility of peace on Earth is not one. She believes that if all people are taught to accept one another's differences and to treat one another with compassion and dignity that peace is possible. While I like her hypothesis, I don't believe it is possible for everyone to accept one another because of the bad things that happen to people. Instead some people let fears and ignorance build and grow into prejudice.

Prejudice is the generator that starts wars. Everyone has the ability to do loving, caring, empathetic things. Everyone also has the ability to do chicken-hearted, jealous, hateful things. I don't believe it is possible to drive out something that is in us so deep. We are animals, after all, and not just animals, but predators—worse than any wolf, cougar, or lion could ever be. Just as it is impossible to subdue all instincts in one of those animals, it is impossible for our anger or fear to disappear.

I'm not saying war is natural and good. I just feel that war will never go away because of human nature, but we should strive for peace just the same. — Willow, 16

This earth cannot have peace because not everybody likes each other. I get in fights because of some problem. The playground lady breaks up the fights. Then the counselor makes us talk about it. Then I'm mad at the counselor because she doesn't solve it in my favor. So how can we have peace on Earth when I can't have peace on the playground?

— Chris, 11

■ ■ ■

Even animals fight for food and plants fight for light that lets them live. I guess it's a fighting world. — David, 11

■ ■ ■

There will always be war because there will always be someone crazy enough to kill. . . . To get rid of all the killers in the world, we ourselves would have to become murderers.

— Tiffany, 17

Hitler and Saddam Hussein must have been teased and pushed around when they were kids and they got mad and wanted to start hurting other people. — Tanner, 11

■ ■ ■

Even if world peace was achieved it would only last for a short while. Then someone would start to fight over who is the most peaceful. — Greg, 15

There could never be peace because of the economy. Every time we go to war more people have jobs, but if we had total peace, the economy would fall and less jobs would be available. If there were no wars the armed forces men and women would be out of jobs. Then the people that have jobs may be laid off because the servicemen/women may have more skills and take their jobs. Every time we have a war it makes people sad because they have relatives that have to fight, but think what would happen if we didn't have wars—people would not have money for Christmas!

War is not a good thing, but we would also have to think about the consequences of having total peace. — T.J., 12

I have two opinions on war. One part hates it because so many soldiers (and people, too) get killed when they almost do not have any opinion about the situation or don't care. When they need people to fight they take people who are barely out of high school.

The other part of me thinks that war is great with all of the guns and tanks and weapons. It's great to watch all of these men and women walk through forests and swamps in camouflage. It's awesome to watch people get blown away, yet it is really sad.

One of my friends is waiting to go to war in Saudi Arabia. I don't want him to go, but if he has to, he has to. — Jess, 13

I am scared, deathly scared, of war. Many members of my family were in a war. My father was in the Vietnam War, my grandpa was in World War II, and my great uncle was in the Korean War. I have seen the casualties and suffering of war and I am frightened to see it happen all over again.

Our world has been at war since the beginning of time and so it will remain until the end of time. — Nate, 13

How can absolutely no war be possible? Even if all the countries are at peace with each other, there is still war. Some ask, "How can this be?"

Ask the thirteen-year-old girl who was raped a block from her home if she is at peace. Ask the parents of the child who was hit and run by a drunk driver if they feel peace. Ask the people in South Africa who are prisoners of apartheid if they are at peace. Ask the homeless man sitting on the street corner if there is no war. Ask the woman who is battered by her husband if there is peace.

Just because armies aren't occupying other countries with tanks and missiles, doesn't mean there is peace. Ask the people.

— Carrie, 16

The way I see it, the day there's peace on Earth, I'll be in heaven watching. — Kory, 11

If God wanted peace on planet Earth, he or she would have made this earth with peace in the first place. — Tammy, 10

One way to have peace on earth is if the gravitational pull stops and everyone flings off the face of the earth into thin air or if somebody blows up the earth and kills everyone except two people. I think two people could live in peace. They wouldn't want to kill or fight each other because then they'd be all alone.

The world has its ups (peace) and its downs (war). Sorry to say we're going down, down, down, down, down!

— Alisa, 11

There will always be some weird person who will cause trouble. The biggest step towards achieving peace is we should get rid of those people or we should put them through counseling.

— Jody, 12

■ ■ ■

The way to stop war is easy. Just respect each other. Not respecting each other starts wars. — Christopher, 7

To stop fighting and have peace I would make a peace school. A peace school is where you go twenty-five minutes more before or after school. Everyone must go. The kids learn not to fight. When they grow up no one will be fighting. Starting with kids is my way to have peace on earth. — Joseph, 9

You could always try to change human nature, but it's very hard to give billions of people lobotomies. — Chloe, 12

I believe that one day, for one moment, there will be peace among everybody. People and animals all over the world will stop fighting and hating and they will think to themselves, "What is the reason for weapons? What are their purposes? Killing? Hurting? What for?" That little voice inside people will take over and people will start to think, "What a wonderful Earth this is." — Benjamin, 9

WONDER

Where does the white go when the snow melts? I would like to know because I'm very curious . . . and it seems like a mystery. — Rachel, 8

ONE ASPECT OF children that sets them apart from most adults is their marvelously unfettered ability to wonder. From their earliest years they begin to ask questions about the people, the world, and the events surrounding them.

Virtually nothing is outside their purview. They want to know why after it rains dead worms are strewn on the sidewalk, who made up swear words, and if magic is real. They ask questions about their futures and their pasts. They wonder if their pets have the same feelings they do and what it would like to be a dolphin or a wild horse. They ask questions about who they are and who they want to be.

They wonder because it's their nature to wonder. "Why do I wonder?" writes Damaris, 11. "Because it's fun and something to do, and always different. Because it belongs only to me. And sometimes, I still wonder why I wonder at all."

We asked children to imagine there's a person who knows everything and can answer any question anyone has. What would their question be? Their responses illuminate the beauty of children's wonder—a wonder that encompasses both the profound and seemingly insignificant, the universal, and the unique.

■ ■ ■

Why was Jesus so poor if he got all those jewels and gold? Why I ask is because I saw the Nativity play and when Jesus was born he was given many riches. When he grew up he was poor just like somebody on the streets. What happened to the jewels and gold? — Jimmy, 11

Why do golfers wear such nutty clothes? — Andy, 10

Why are there girls? I don't understand why there are girls. Sometimes they are a bother and a pest. — Colin, 10

I would ask this person this: What's the weather going to be like tomorrow? Why? So I know what to wear. — Amy, 10

■ ■ ■

Do you think I'm going to be a cake decorator? I want to know so I could practice making roses. — Mary Kay, 11

How can I be an animal lover if I am a hunter? I love squirrels and I hunt squirrels. The same with rabbits. I have not killed anything yet, but if I could shoot straight I would kill one. Why would I if I really love animals? — Matt, 9

If I were to ask one question it would be, "How did God create humans?" This is a question I've wondered all my life. How did he? Did he just think or say "humans"? Did he just think it up and make us with one sweep of his hand? Or was it just a mixture of chemicals?

The reason I chose this question out of all other questions is because if we knew how we were created, maybe more people would accept that God made everyone equally. If everyone believed that, we would probably have a more peaceful world.
— Anne, 10

If I could ask you anything it would be how do I become a better piano player. Why? Because I stink at piano. — Maria, 9

What college did you go to? Because then I could go there, too. — Nick, 12

I would ask who is going to win the World Series because then I would know what baseball cards to collect and what autographs to get. — Ryan, 8

I would ask how many people are there in the world so I could subtract from the people I know and see how many people I don't know. I think it will be a challenge to get to know thirty people each year. — Kyle, 9

What is love? I would ask this question because I have met so many people who could not explain love very easily. I also think that knowing what love is would give you a lot of wisdom.
— Katinha, 11

What happened to my cat, Pumpkin, after he left? My reason for picking this question is that he was my favorite cat, and I want to know if he found a loving home. — Theresa, 11

Why do mothers cry over something on television? I would ask this because it's only a story and it's usually not true!!!
— Jason, 9

If I had one question to ask, I would ask the Lord. The question would be: What were you doing with Moses all that time besides telling and giving him the Ten Commandments? I'd ask him that because I want to know what God talks to people about in private conversations. — Craig, 10

Why is it that your parents will ground you or say you can't go someplace and say they did it because they love you? Because most of the time it doesn't seem like they are telling the truth. If they do love us so much, then why don't they let us go have fun and be happy? — Carrie, 11

Is there really a Loch Ness monster? I would like to know because if I ever go swimming then I know not to go swimming in that lake. — Denise, 10

■ ■ ■

Why can't third-graders drive cars? Why I want to know is because I want to drive right now. — Tommy, 9

I want to know who was the first person to get the chicken pox. You have to get the chicken pox from somebody. Everybody gets the chicken pox once or twice. I have always wondered, who got the chicken pox first? — Andrea, 8

How come my brother is older than me? I want to be older than my brother. — Molly, 7

Are my parents going to live a full life? The reason why I'm asking this question is because they have gotten me everything I ever wanted. They are there every time I have a problem. They do not get mad when I do something wrong. I love them very much and I want them to live forever. — Brian, 10

Who am I going to get married to? I would want to know that because I would want to see if she is pretty or not. I always wanted to know that. I sure hope she doesn't smoke or my dad would be mad at me. — Josh, 11

■ ■ ■

I would ask when the world will explode because I don't want to be around when it does. — Brandi, 12

Is it easier being a child or a grown-up? I want to know that because I want to know if I should be enjoying life right now or be looking forward to life in the future. — Renee, 11